\$3

A Year of Spirituality

A YEAR OF SPIRITUALITY

a seasonal guide to new awareness

Ingrid Collins

**Andrews McMeel
Publishing**

Kansas City

First published by MQ Publications Limited
12 The Ivories
6–8 Northampton Street
London N1 2HY

Series Editor: Ljiljana Baird
Designer: Tracy Timson
Illustrator: Penny Brown

ISBN: 0-7407-3018-5
Library of Congress Control Number: 2002111877
03 04 05 06 07 PAR 10 9 8 7 6 5 4 3 2 1

ATTENTION: Schools and Businesses
Andrews McMeel books are available at quantity discounts with bulk purchase for educational,
business, or sales promotional use. For information, please write to: Special Sales Department,
Andrews McMeel Publishing, 4520 Main Street, Kansas City, Missouri 64111.

This book is written for all those interested in the area of spirituality and healing.
It is not an attempt to diagnose or treat specific conditions. If readers are in any doubt about
their health they should seek appropriate professional advice, especially in cases of persistent
pain or other continuing symptoms. The publisher and the author of this book take
no responsibility for the reader's health or use or misuse of the information contained herein.

Contents

Introduction

To see a World in a Grain of Sand
And a Heaven in a Wild Flower,
Hold Infinity in the palm of your hand
And Eternity in an hour.

From "Auguries of Innocence" by WILLIAM BLAKE

Spirituality can be accessed everywhere, at any time, and in all the seasons—in the home and the workplace as well as in the monastery, in fair weather or when the snow lies glistening and deep on the ground. This practical book offers spiritual techniques that help enrich your every moment, transforming familiar actions into extraordinary experiences, enlarging your awareness, and illuminating your days with the joy that is your birthright.

You will not have to sit at the feet of gurus, masters, priests, or intercessors of any kind to create your own intimate and sacred moments. Rooted in ordinary circumstances, and throughout the familiar seasonal flow of life, you too can experience time-slips into spirituality, discover what the true alignment should be in your physical, emotional, and spiritual existence, or, at the very least, simply enjoy who you are and what you are doing in your life in new and blissful ways.

We are all physically, emotionally, and spiritually linked to the seasons, each of which has a particular energy and attraction. *A Year of Spirituality* follows the traditional Feng Shui divisions of the year and the qualities associated with each season—emergence, illumination, gathering, and nourishment—to build a program of transformational awareness.

Your mind is a miraculous doorway into spiritual insights, opening and leading you into the domain of the soul. Often on this year's journey you will find exercises that use the mind to lead you into spiritual understandings, enriching your entire being at every level of existence. Whatever your religion, and even if you have none, this book will, I hope, augment your familiarity with Spirit, the fundamental essence of being alive and connected to all life.

I have planted flowers in the form of folktales, fairy stories, and legends along the way, because of their inspirational qualities and their capacity to shed light on problems that challenge us as much as they did our ancestors. These legends resonate with deep meanings for communities trying to understand the significance of the natural world. Inherited by us from spiritually aware peoples throughout the ages, they are as potent now as when they first emerged from some gifted storyteller's imagination.

When embarking on the many meditations and visualizations in this book I suggest you take up the pharaoh position, so-called because Ancient Egyptian rulers used it. Sit in a comfortable, upright, high-backed armchair with your arms supported on its armrests and with both feet firmly on the ground. In this position, no two parts of your body touch, and so you do not give yourself confusing messages of physical contact. You are therefore less aware of your body and more able to focus on your inner being—your soul—and its innate wisdom.

When choosing a good space in which to meditate, place yourself at least four feet away from any electrical equipment. With your eyes closed you can access your imagination without the hindrance of external visual stimuli and if, prior to relaxing into a visualization or meditation, you turn off all the gadgets of modern living (for example your telephones), then environmental sound stimuli will not intrude into your inner world. Research has shown that we learn best from our own voice, so if you record yourself reading aloud the passages of visualization and meditation in this book, it will be easier to relax and follow the instructions.

Before you do anything else, make or buy a notebook. This is to be your Spirit Diary in which to record spiritual insights gained and new connections and understandings discovered throughout the year. Make your Spirit Diary as physically beautiful as you can, using all your creativity with colors, textures, and possibly perfumes, and on its first pages write, draw, paint, or use collage to describe some of the everyday miracles around you. At the end of each story, exercise, visualization, or meditation, make an entry in your Spirit Diary describing your personal reactions, thoughts, and insights gained.

The most effective way to consolidate your learning is to teach someone your newly acquired knowledge, so ask someone close to you (call this person your Soul Friend) to sit down with you and listen to what you have gained from each month's exercises, stories, meditations, and visualizations. Alternatively, if you would prefer a more private form of reflection on your learning, think of your Soul Friend as your Higher Self, that part of your soul that only wishes yourself well and that is connected to the highest point in the universe. Look upon your Higher Self as an invisible being who is always on your wavelength, totally trustworthy, and supportive of your spiritual goals.

I wish you a wondrous journey and joy of this book.

EMERGING

Life has its own rhythms and circles. Just as the seasons flow one into the next in the miracle of existence, so life emerges in this season to begin its journey through birth, maturity, procreation, age, and finally death, which makes way for the creation of new life once more.

From the time when the first white snowdrop forces its leaves up through the rich brown earth, we are reminded of the promised feast of life. It is as if you can hear the vigorous green leaves unfurl and greet the pale spring sky, sighing as they take their place in the sun. Their waxy sweet perfume is filled with the promise of good things to come, and we look forward to our year's adventure, our journey of spiritual development.

At the start of the life cycle, fish swim purposefully to their breeding pools, frogs return to familiar places to spawn, and birds, some having flown long distances from their winter homelands, return with their mates to their old nests to repair the ravages of winter. All is in readiness for the process of procreation that lies ahead, which renews the world with regenerating life. We, too, must awake from our dream of separateness to understand that we are all connected in Spirit, making that transformational step into spiritual consciousness, the metaphysical reality that is the oneness of all creation.

MONTH

1

Birth and the feminine principle

Letting go of sadness and anger

Choosing to change your attitude

Creation myths

Birth and the feminine principle

Spring is traditionally the woman's time, the time for germination and gestation. The season's significant images are female, representing the creative Spirit that is within both men and women. Whether or not the female icon is associated with motherhood, her presence draws attention to the power and importance of female creativity in our lives. A parallel is seen in Mother Earth, who gives new life to animals and plants.

The purity and piety of some female icons represent the dedication to the creative process. We find these appearing in most cultures. In the Hindu pantheon, Parvati is the goddess wife of Siva, the god of destruction and regeneration. She gives life to Ganesh, god of wisdom and the remover of all obstacles, by fashioning him from earth and sprinkling water from a sacred river over him. Gnostics worshiped Sophia (Wisdom), the female aspect of their deity, who was capable of independent creation. For Christians, the Virgin Mary represents the purity and unconditional nature of a mother's love, while Mary Magdalene represents the earthly pleasure of physical love. In Mahayana Buddhism, the youthful image of Green Tara is seen as a female bodhisattva whose color represents vigor and activity. Followers of Islam highly revere and ascribe great status to the mother's role within the family, for her fecundity and her care of the youngsters. The world over, humankind meditates on the power of Mother Earth and ascribes mystical properties to the processes of pregnancy and birth. Countless myths of creation abound in all cultures.

Persephone and Demeter

The Ancient Greek myth of Persephone and her mother, Demeter, the goddess of the earth, explains the natural cycle of growth and decay to which all life is subject. A virginal and beautiful divinity, Persephone attracted the love of Aidoneus, the god of the underworld, who captured her and imprisoned her below the earth until she would agree to be his wife. Demeter was distraught and would not allow anything to grow or blossom until her grief was assuaged and her daughter returned.

Faced with devastating famine, the gods tried to persuade Aidoneus to release Persephone. He agreed, but before she left he tempted her to eat three pomegranate seeds—this fruit being a symbol of marriage. Aidoneus declared that this was an indication that Persephone also wanted to be with him and insisted that she remain with him for three months of every year—one month for every seed she had eaten. So every winter Persephone descends into the underworld and the earth mourns with her mother, but in the spring she comes back and Demeter allows life to return to the world for another nine months.

15

Letting go of sadness and anger

In eating the pomegranate seeds, Persephone reacts in a familiar way to being trapped in a personal hell of unhappiness—over time she becomes attached to unhappiness, out of habit, or fear of unknown alternatives. We are often drawn to the things we fear or that give us pain. In *The Prophet*, Kahlil Gibran describes Almustafa leaving the city of Orphalese:

But as he descended the hill, a sadness came upon him, and he thought in his heart:

How shall I go in peace and without sorrow? Nay, not without a wound in the spirit shall I leave this city.

Long were the days of pain I have spent within its walls, and long were the nights of aloneness; and who can depart from his pain and his aloneness without regret?

Too many fragments of the spirit have I scattered in these streets, and too many are the children of my longing that walk naked among these hills, and I cannot withdraw from them without a burden and an ache.

It is not a garment I cast off this day, but a skin that I tear with my own hands.

Nor is it a thought I leave behind me, but a heart made sweet with hunger and thirst.

Gibran also talks of the process of breaking out from our pain and describes it as enclosing our understanding:

Even as a stone of a fruit must break, that its heart may stand in the sun, so must you know pain.

And could you keep your heart in wonder at the daily miracles of your life, your pain would not seem less wondrous than your joy;

And you would accept the seasons of your heart, even as you have always accepted the seasons that pass over your fields.

And you would watch with serenity through the winters of your grief.

Do you have any painful areas in your life that could be likened to a personal Hades, from which you yearn to emerge—even though a small part of you is fascinated enough to remain? Until you let go of your interest you will struggle to make significant progress. Letting go of your sadness and anger is a lovely exercise to do in the first month of spring because it is good to clear the slate before you dive headlong into the year ahead. With the newfound clarity that it brings you will be free to embrace positive new experiences and choose your direction without old fears and resentments encumbering you.

The Girl in the Silk Kimono

A Zen story tells of two monks who were walking the long distance from one monastery to another and who, on reaching a crossroads, found a pretty young woman in distress. There had been a torrential rainstorm and the ground was very muddy. The woman was crying because she had to cross the junction, but to do so would mean that the swampy rivers of mud would ruin the beautiful silk kimono she was wearing. One of the monks picked her up in his arms and carried her across the road, gently putting her down safely on the other side. The woman, now very happy, thanked him profusely.

The two monks carried on their journey in silence, reached their monastery, bathed, robed, and ate their supper before the second monk burst into angry accusations. "I'm surprised and horrified at you!" he exploded. "You know that in our brotherhood we are not allowed to talk to a woman, let alone physically take her into our arms! What were you thinking of?"

The first monk answered with a smile, "My dear brother! I put her down immediately on the other side of the road. What rage has caused you to have been carrying her all the way here?"

Write down all the things you are sad or angry about in your life. Imagine wrapping them in a beautiful silk kimono. Now carry them to the other side of the road and leave them there.

The figure of eight

This method of healing old arguments or tidying up unfinished business with someone who you might have been carrying like the monk in the story derives its name from the shape of the number eight, or two touching circles. When emerging from this visualization, many people experience a newfound sense of peace, forgiveness, and liberation.

* Sitting in your high-backed armchair in the meditative pharaoh position (see page 8), let your imagination take you on a journey through either a beautiful turquoise- or violet-colored cloud to a safe space. This could be a place where you remember feeling safe, or you might like to create a new room in your imagination.

* Look around you until you find a place to sit down in complete comfort. Invite the person with whom you have unfinished business to come in and sit with you. Draw a figure of eight around you both, so that you are sitting in two touching circles.

* Tell this person everything that is within your heart that you need to say, however difficult or painful it might be, and when you have finished, tell yourself "Yes."

* Now listen while the person tells you everything that they need to say, however difficult or painful it might be for you to hear it, and, when you have finished listening, tell yourself "Yes."

20

* Now that you have exchanged your thoughts with each other, look down into your hands and see your gift for the other person. It is an object that is significant to you and necessary for you to give for healing to take place. What is it? What does it represent?

* As you give your gift, look into the other person's hands at their gift for you. It is an object that is significant to you both and necessary for you to receive for healing to take place. What is it? What does it represent?

* Now be aware that very fine silver strands connect your body to that of the other person. Take a pair of golden scissors—gold is one of the highest-level colors—and, when you have cut every single thread, tell yourself "Yes."

* From the ground within the two circles in which you are both sitting there emerges a brilliant azure light (calming and healing the red of anger and antagonism), until it has risen about one and a half feet above your heads. Now you and the other person are sitting in two touching cylinders of blue light.

* Separate the two cylinders, put a magic lid on each, and open your eyes, so that now both you and the other person are no longer entangled or enmeshed. You are both free.

* When you are ready, come gently back from that place through your favorite color, into the room and open your eyes.

Choosing to change your attitude

It is important to be able to detach yourself from emotive situations so that you are liberated from immediate meanings and their emotional consequences; then you can more easily and freely choose how to feel. While it is not always possible to change your situation, you can change the way you relate to it and, therefore, at what spiritual level you are able to make your important life-choices. Even deep tragedy can be valued as the gift of a learning experience. Sometimes the greatest gifts come wrapped in the most unlikely packages. Write down some of the events in your life that you consider to be causes of sadness. Look beneath the obviousness of the tragedy until you find what pieces of positive wisdom you have learned about yourself and your life that you could not have known without this experience.

Setting and achieving your goals

As the new year begins we usually set out with lots of good intentions and resolutions. Make a list of your goals in the order of their importance. Maybe you want to give more time to your children or your parents, or renew old and valued friendships. Your partner may need you to demonstrate your love a little more, or you might want to embark on an adventurous new project at work. If you truly want something then you have to believe it can happen.

Positive outcomes

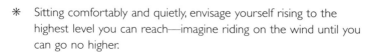

To ensure that the bountiful universe helps us to fulfill our goals, we are going to visualize them being successfully achieved in the future. When that time comes they are more likely to be attained.

* Sitting comfortably and quietly, envisage yourself rising to the highest level you can reach—imagine riding on the wind until you can go no higher.

* From this position view the year ahead. See each of your goals being realized in the best possible way for all concerned. Now imagine all the people who will be in your life to love you and be loved by you, to share mutual support and encouragement.

* Now travel into the future, seeing only beneficial scenarios for all the people involved. Greet everyone whose life you intend to enrich in the coming year. When you have warmly greeted them, let your imagination ride high with theirs through to the end of the year.

* Thank them for a brilliant journey, as gratitude is a health-giving emotion. Then return to the here and now, refreshed and ready for a superb year.

Wise Farmer, Wild Horse

This ancient story underlines the importance of being detached from events.

A wild horse one day appeared and made its home in a farmer's field. "How lucky you are to have acquired such a fine horse for nothing!" said his neighbors. "Maybe, maybe not," replied the farmer. The farmer's son, who was his only helping hand around the farm, tried to ride the horse. It threw him, breaking his legs. "How unlucky for you," chorused the neighbors. "Maybe, maybe not," replied the farmer. The young man was left behind when the emperor's soldiers arrived in the village to conscript all the able-bodied young men into the army, many of whom were to die in the war. Meanwhile, the farmer's wild horse ran away. "How unfortunate!" cried his neighbors. "Maybe, maybe not," rejoined the farmer. The horse returned to his field bringing his entire herd with him. "What good fortune!" exclaimed his neighbors. "Maybe, maybe not," reflected the wise farmer.

The green energy of a new beginning

Light green is the color associated with spring in the natural world. Green is found at the center of the visible spectrum of light energy, and therefore has a centering effect, bringing balance to your emotional life. Therefore, by immersing yourself in the color green, you will become finely attuned to emergent life and more aware of what is happening in the natural world around you.

* Sitting comfortably in the pharaoh position (see page 8), observe your breathing. Notice how intelligent your body is, knowing just what sort of breaths to take—deep or shallow, fast or slow. Be aware that you are the one who is the breather of your breaths.

* Imagine the pale green color of new leaves as they emerge from the ground. Surround yourself in this new growing green, imagining how this color would taste, what perfume it might have, how it would feel to the touch, and of what music it reminds you.

* Take three deep breaths, concentrating your attention on the out-breath, and imagine bathing your body inside and out with this beautiful color.

* Return gently to full present consciousness and open your eyes.

Creation myths

Exploring stories about creation from different cultures helps us to distill meaning from the unknown so that we can find spiritual sense in our surroundings. In the Judeo-Christian tradition, God made the world in six days and rested on the seventh. He separated light from darkness, the dry land from the sea, the heavens from the earth, and created all living things, which He gave into the care of humankind. He created the first woman, Eve, from the rib of the first man, Adam. When they became presumptuous enough to eat the forbidden fruit from the tree of knowledge, God banished Adam and Eve from the Garden of Eden and they became forever outcasts, dreaming of a return to paradise.

As in most ancient cultures, the Egyptians created myths to help them to explain their existence and to understand nature. Their creation myths are about the deities of the earth, the sky, the sun, the moon, the stars, and, of course, the Nile, which floods its banks every year, bringing fertility to the soil. The Ancient Egyptians thought water to be fundamental to the notion of creation. In one of their myths the world was generated from chaotic churning water called Nu. Out of the bubbling inundation emerged a pyramid-shaped hill of dry land, and to this first hilltop on the first day came the first sunrise. After this came many more hills and from these dry lands the world emerged. The creator god or rising sun was called Khepri, the great scarab beetle. He was known also as Ra-Harakhte, seen as a winged solar disk, changing to the strong Ra at midday and the old man Atum, or Horus, on the horizon at sunset.

Find your favorite creation myth. This could be a legend or sacred story from your own culture, or a tale that has always entranced you. Re-create it in your own words and write it in your Spirit Diary (see page 8), illustrating it with whatever images and techniques you choose.

Next, ask family members, friends, and colleagues about their favorite creation stories. Make a collection of these legends, find the commonality of the themes, and then create a new story of your own, with powerful images of the fecundity of life emerging into the physical world from the barren winter landscapes.

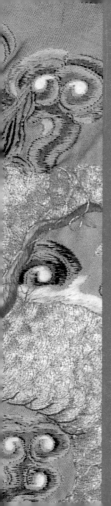

MONTH

2

Soul awareness

Nurturing your existence

Exploring the relationship between body, mind, and soul

Making positive life choices

Regarding work as a spiritual process

Soul awareness

Energy is the force of life that is ever present in the world. It gives you blueprints for your goals, powers your thoughts, holds memories of your experiences, and stimulates you and all living things to grow, learn, progress, laugh, and love. At its most subtle level it is the stuff of your soul and of the Spirit World.

In the second month of your nascent journey, we will be emerging into an awareness of this life force. We will introduce ourselves to the sensation of our own spiritual energy and begin to use this in the service of our own health and the well-being of those around us. Just as a tiny lamp sends out its light into the darkness, and that light can travel (if unobstructed) for eternity, so we can take onboard the idea that our spiritual energy, the equivalent of our light, is potentially limitless and is not separate from all of eternal creation. This cosmic idea has implications for us as we become increasingly aware of our spirituality. When we give positive energy of good thoughts, deeds, and intentions into the universe, we raise the positive level of energy and so we, too, being part of the universe, benefit from that improved spiritual environment.

The aura

In the last century, a Russian electrical engineer, Simeon Kirlian, and his wife developed a photographic method of recording the force field that exists around all living things. Clairvoyants, the name given to those who can see the field unaided, describe it as a moving sea of colors around a person, animal, or plant, which they term the aura. They are able to perceive a fine energy field even after the death of the physical body, separate from and independent of the body. The aura consists of spiritual energy, and people who work with Spirit regard this as the essential part of a person—the soul. Animals and plants also have auras, and through Kirlian photography we see that even if a plant's leaf is cut or in some way mutilated, its aura remains intact.

The power of thought energy

Kirlian images also confirm that when growing, a plant throws out an energy field matrix in the shape of a leaf from its stem at the growing point before the physical leaf grows into it. In Month 1, the positive outcomes visualization (see page 23) was a way of projecting a spiritual energy matrix of good thoughts into our future, making it easier for their physical manifestation to take place. This makes Henry Ford's famous quote "Whether you think you can or you can't, you're absolutely right!" understandable on a spiritual level.

Nurturing your existence

There are three aspects of existence: the body, mind, and soul. In everyday life we tend to pay attention to the needs of our physical bodies—warming ourselves when we are cold, feeding ourselves when we are hungry, drinking when we are thirsty, working when we need to earn the means to sustain ourselves, sleeping when we are tired, making love when we are romantically and sexually excited by our partners, and so on. We are living in a physical world that derives its energy from the sun. All living things need the light and warmth of the sun to grow, to stay alive, and to stay healthy.

Then we have a mind and emotional system that exists within a network of relationships and core beliefs, whose energy source is our thoughts and feelings. If we have sadness, upsets, trauma, or loss in our lives, then we lose emotional energy and may become emotionally unwell or ill at ease. In the emerging field of medical knowledge called psychoneuro-immunology, practitioners are beginning to refer to the body and the mind as one entity, the bodymind, to reflect the intimate connection between physical and emotional energy.

Our spiritual body is there, too, and has its own source of energy, which we can draw on to alter our emotional and physical states of health. Just as people and places exist in the physical world and can contribute to our happiness and well-being should we wish to avail ourselves of them, so in the dimension of spiritual energy there is a source available to us for living, healing, and promoting enlightenment. This is the fount of every subtle, spiritual phenomenon in the universe. It is the cosmic life force.

Bart Simpson Sells His Soul

In one episode of The Simpsons, Matt Groening's cult animation for television, Bart Simpson, the son of the family, decides to earn easy money by selling his soul for five bucks to a classmate at school. He writes "Bart's soul" on a piece of paper and swaps it for the cash. He feels very pleased with himself, as he believes that he has conned his friend out of his money, but on returning home he finds that his dog, who always barks a joyous welcome for him, ignores him completely. He goes to a building that has automatic doors, and the doors do not open for him. Bart learns the hard way that the real, recognizable presence that we know to be a person is the energy of the soul.

Aura awareness

This exercise has three parts. The first two parts encourage you to feel and see the energy around your hands so that you will become increasingly aware of your own aura. The third part enables you to demonstrate to yourself that the aura is strengthened by the energy of loving thoughts. You will come to the unavoidable understanding that when you have love in your heart you become stronger; the aura is the essential aspect of the being that is you. When this marvelous strength energizes your life, you benefit from increased well-being—both emotional and physical—as do all those who are connected to you.

Part 1

* Sit comfortably in the pharaoh position (see page 8) in a favorite place in your home.

* Stretch out your arms on both sides of your body.

* Keeping your upper body relaxed, bring your hands toward each other as if you were starting to clap in slow motion.

* Hold the position when you begin to feel a slight resistance in the air between your hands—a slight pressure, a tingling feeling, or a warmth before they physically touch. What you are feeling is the energy of the aura.

36

Part 2

✳ Stretch out one hand, with fingers spread wide, against a very light nonpatterned background so that you can view the back of your hand clearly.

✳ View the hand and background as if they were on the same plane, with no distance between them. You might be able to perceive a light surrounding your hand that moves simultaneously with your hand as you alter its position. This light does not trail behind the hand as an optical effect of a dark object against a light background would.

✳ Try the same exercise against a dark, nonpatterned background and determine which shows the energy of your aura more clearly.

Part 3

✳ Now bring into your mind the memory of a person, animal, or place that you deeply love. Feel that love welling up into your heart and then, stretching out your arms, send that love from your heart through your arms and feel it tingle as it leaves your fingers on its way to the loved one.

✳ After a few minutes of powerfully sending your love to a loved one, relax and then repeat the aura awareness exercises above. You will find that the process of allowing your love to flow has increased the strength of your aura, the outwardly tangible area of your soul.

Exploring the relationship between body, mind, and soul

The soul and the physical body are connected but do not consist of the same matter. It is possible to become aware, from the viewing position of your soul, of your physical body. You think tens of thousands of thoughts every day, but the majority of them are the same as you thought yesterday. You instruct your body how to breathe, your mind how to take up an attitude, and your immune system how to function—you can influence the functions of your body from the powerhouse of your thoughts. For example, if you think of the taste of a particularly juicy lemon, your mouth begins to water, the energy of thought having influenced your physical digestive system. If you were to stop thinking and simply observe your body from the center of your soul, allowing there to be a gap between body and soul, you would permit your body to return to the natural harmony it was born with. And it is from harmony that well-being springs.

Breathing awareness

The following meditation comes from the ayurvedic
tradition of Indian mysticism. Among its benefits is a
deep feeling of peace and balance on returning to the
normal state of consciousness.

* Sitting comfortably in the pharaoh position (see page 8), and having created as quiet an environment as possible, prepare to spend approximately fifteen minutes on this meditation.

* Innocently turn your attention to your breathing. Notice how intelligent your body is—it knows just what breaths to take.

* Now innocently turn your attention to yourself, the breather of your breaths, the thinker of your thoughts, and be aware of the energy and intelligence that is you.

* Be aware of your uniqueness and your connectedness to all life before returning to the here and now, stretching like a cat, feeling fully present and alert.

Making positive life choices

We often hear people talk about the joys of spring, and indeed these early months of the year can be particularly blissful. Just as it is important to start each day by choosing to be happy, so it is essential when surrounded by so much evidence of nature's new beginnings to remind ourselves of the state of joy that is available to each of us and of the enormous potential of fresh energy that surrounds us.

Recalling joy

You may find by doing this exercise that you remember all sorts of wonderful things that you had forgotten in the course of your busy life.

* Write a list of every happy person you have known in your life, and a few ideas about why they are happy. Note the times you were in these people's company, when you laughed with them, and what you laughed about.

* What characteristics of these people can be a model for you? If they found themselves in difficult situations, how would they choose to regain their feelings of happiness?

* At the end of each day, remember how many times you smiled or laughed. Did you, by a kind or funny gesture, make someone else smile or laugh, too?

Walk through to happiness

Robert Holden, director of the Happiness Project in Oxford, UK, teaches this exercise. If you follow the instructions through to the end, you need never be tempted to feel that you are an unfortunate, unhappy victim of the tyranny of sadness.

* Imagine three large circles in a line on the floor. The first circle contains all the reasons that you consider give you happiness. The second circle contains all the reasons that you consider are blocking the way to your being happy. The third circle is the space of pure joy, where all the blissful energy of the universe exists.

* Choose to step into the first circle and feel all those happy reasons bubbling up around you, as if you were standing in a glass of champagne! Enjoy the feeling. Celebrate the existence of all these reasons that you consider give you happiness.

* Now choose to step into the second circle. Remember that the best gifts in the world often come in the shabbiest packaging. Sometimes, by rising to a particularly difficult challenge, we become aware of our amazing resilience or our compassionate nature. And we always take with us some special learning that enriches us for life's future challenges. Let the reasons that you consider are blocking the way to your being happy bubble up in front of you. As each one appears, unpack it and find the special gift it has brought you.

*   Finally, choose to step into the third circle of pure, cosmic joy. This is a joy that needs no reasons, unreasonable joy purely for joy's sake. It exists simply because you know it to be there and available to you. Let yourself experience this totally blissful feeling. You have chosen to make this step into happiness. Standing here, turn and look back at the first two circles, and see how different they look when you know you have a choice, and how much stronger you feel when in charge of your own emotions.

*   Write in your Spirit Diary how this exercise has empowered your ability to choose cosmic joy and how the first two circles look when viewed from the perspective of the third circle.

Patch Adams

The story of Hunter "Patch" Adams is inspirational. Patch and his colleagues at the Gesundheit! Institute are doctors, clowns, and heroes. Patch assumes that soldiers won't shoot clowns, and that policemen won't use their truncheons on clowns, so he leads his colleagues into war-torn countries, into hospital wards full of dying children, bringing laughter into their lives. His father was a soldier who died at the time that the United States was involved in Vietnam, when Patch was sixteen. Patch was so devastated by the waste of human life in war and his awareness of worldwide human suffering, that at first he could not cope. By the age of eighteen he had been hospitalized three times with severe depression. Then he made a choice. He could look forward to a life in psychiatric institutions or he could dedicate his life to optimism and to the service of health, peace, and happiness of humanity. Patch Adams does not consider himself a hero: he says that feeling as he does, it would take courage not to act the way he does.

An optimist wakes up, gets out of bed, draws the curtains, and says, "Good morning, God!" A pessimist, however, when drawing back the curtain, groans, "Good God! Morning!" You can be in tune with the optimism and joy of spring simply by making the choice to be happy every morning.

Regarding work as a spiritual process

Just as Patch Adams chose his work because of his convictions, so you, too, can choose to express the goodness of your soul through the paid and voluntary work you do. We all have the power to bring joy and spiritual light into the workplace. As you finish your day's work, think how you have served your colleagues, clients, patients, or customers today. What positive acts did you contribute to their well-being?

The flying geese principle

A flock of geese flies in a V formation, with one goose at the head of the V. For many years it was assumed that this goose was the strongest, the leader of the flock. Now, through aerial photography, ornithologists have discovered that the leading goose creates a current of air that buoys up the ones behind, making it easier for them to fly. They, in turn, create more air currents for the next goose, and so on down the line. When the leader becomes tired, it falls behind and another takes its position. By sharing the burden of leadership, all successfully reach their destination.

* Visualize yourself as part of that flock of geese. Feel how good it is to fly in cooperation with the others. Take the lead when you feel strong, and allow others to take your place when you need a rest.

MONTH

3

Love

In the third month of our journey, the late spring sunshine grows increasingly warm, heating our tender feelings for each other. Love is said to blossom in spring and, as the season draws to a close, love is traditionally given expression and celebrated in the form of marriages.

What is love? People have been attempting to answer this question for thousands of years, but love's ineffable, mystical quality eludes satisfactory definition. Whatever the definition, though, it is the bridge over which spiritual healing flows, and the most exhilarating connection that people can experience. In the aura awareness exercises of last month (see page 36), we saw how love can strengthen the energy of our auras. Love is an energy source originating in Spirit. We can choose to be open to receive it or we can ignore it. If we ignore it we cut off an essential part of ourselves, because unconditional spiritual love enhances the energy of life, the energy of being, the energy of the soul.

In the 1960s a whole generation applauded the Beatles when they sang, "All you need is love."

Sophocles wrote in 406 B.C.E. in *Oedipus Coloneus:* "One word / Frees us of all the weight and pain of life: that word is love."

Lope de Vega in *Fuenteovejuna,* in 1613, wrote, "Harmony is pure love, for love is complete agreement."

In the book *The Little Prince,* written in 1943, Antoine de Saint-Exupéry says: "It is only with the heart that one can see rightly; what is essential is invisible to the eye."

C. G. Jung, the pioneering analyst, once said: "Where love rules, there is no will to power."

Umberto Maturana, systemic philosopher and biological scientist, defines love as "The biological stickiness."

Physical life on this earth is a miraculous opportunity to learn and to communicate about unconditional love, goodness, beauty, and compassion. In the story of the Snow Queen, the evil queen abducts a young boy and freezes his emotions into hard, icy feelings. His adoring sister undertakes the long and arduous journey to rescue him. On discovering him and realizing the damage the Snow Queen has inflicted by the removal of love, the young girl cries. Her tears fall on her brother's eyes and the energy of love in her tears releases the queen's icicles from his eyes, allowing him to recover his ability to give and receive love again.

Plato's *Symposium* tells that once, many years ago, we were very powerful creatures, as powerful as all the gods of Olympus. We had two heads, eight limbs, and a big, thick, strong body. The gods sliced us in two because we challenged their supremacy, and we became the weak creatures that we are today. However, if we are fortunate enough to find our other half and in love are reunited as one, then we regain our power and once again become as strong as any god.

Sleeping Beauty

This traditional fairy tale is universally popular because of the central character's long winter sleep before being found by love and wakened like spring wakens the flowers of the earth.

Once upon a time there lived a king and a queen who longed for an heir. One happy day, their wish was granted: they had a beautiful baby at last! They decided to celebrate by throwing a party for all the people in their kingdom.

The lords and ladies came, bringing fine jewels, gold, and silver as presents for the child. The peasants arrived with articles lovingly woven, carved, and constructed by their own hands. The king and queen had also invited twelve fairies to the party, completely forgetting in their excitement that there were, in fact, thirteen fairies living in the kingdom.

After the lords, ladies, and peasants had given their presents, the twelve fairies fluttered and hovered around the royal cradle, eager as the mortals to offer their gifts. As you may know, fairy gifts are qualities, positive attributes of the body, mind, and soul. They laughed and skipped happily in the air around the baby's head as they showered their gifts: "You shall be gentle," "You shall have the ability to ease people's pain," and so on. The smallest fairy had to wait until last to give her gift, because her eleven brothers and sisters kept knocking her out of the way in their excitement.

When the eleven fairies had finished giving their magical presents to the baby, the littlest fairy had her chance. She flew gently over the baby's heart and raised her wand. But before she could speak the doors were flung open with a crash and in stormed the thirteenth fairy. Everyone gasped and drew back as she shouted at the king and queen, "You unthinking, ignorant people! You will never forget me again. I am going to give your child a present to remember!" She flew to the cradle, casting a dark shadow over the infant and, raising her wand and aiming it venomously at the baby, yelled, "With all your earthly riches, and with all your qualities and positive attributes, you will live on this earth until your sixteenth birthday. On that day you will prick your finger on a spindle and die!" With that, she flew away and was never seen again.

Everyone was devastated. Eventually the king, though completely distraught and numb with despair, became aware of a small being tugging at his sleeve. Through his tears, he looked down and saw the littlest fairy. He bent down so that he could hear her tiny voice above the noise of everyone's sorrow. "Your Majesty," she said, "I'm only small and so my magic is not too strong, but as I haven't given my gift yet I can use my magic to modify the curse." With that she flew to the baby and, with iridescent light showering from her wand as she directed it lovingly at the child, she said sweetly, "I'm afraid that on your sixteenth birthday you will have to prick your finger—I can't change that—but instead of death, sleep will bless you for a hundred years, until at last you will be awakened by a kiss. All those who love you will sleep, too."

And so it came to pass that the beautiful child pricked a finger on a spindle at the age of sixteen and fell into a deep sleep. A thorny, impenetrable forest grew up around the castle, until, a hundred years later, a determined prince full of love turned the thorny hedge into roses with a touch of his sword and awoke the beautiful soul with a loving kiss.

Exercise

Loving Yourself

* You are that beautiful child. You have been sleeping throughout a hundred-year winter, and your castle has been neglected. The rough thorns have grown around in a high, thick hedge to protect you but have also obscured your own view of your real, beautiful soul. It is now time to feel the kiss that awakens you to your true self, and once again take your place in the sun. Celebrate your being present in the world! What were the eleven wonderful qualities and attributes that the fairies gave you at birth? Make a list of them, and pin it somewhere where you can easily see it every morning. Be sure to read it aloud to yourself at least once a day, because we learn most easily from the sound of our own voice.

Science and spirituality

At this stage of our exploration, it is interesting to consider the connection that has recently been made between theories of quantum physics and ancient mysticism. Until now, mystics and scientists could not find a single point of contact or agreement. Now, quantum physicists are discovering that the building bricks of physical matter, atoms, are made up of subatomic particles that exist in states both of matter and energy waves. It is thought that they tend to oscillate between these two states within nanoseconds. Interestingly, if the physicist looks at the particles to find matter, that is what is seen; if energy is looked for, then that is what is seen. The observer influences the observed. Information is recorded onto the particles in the form of energy waves (rather like microscopic audio- or videotape recordings), so that atoms can be regarded as consisting of energy and information, in constant motion.

Mystics have always spoken of vibrations as being a central idea in the transmission of spiritual energy. Now scientists are becoming interested in exploring the effectiveness of spiritual energy phenomena such as healing. Some interesting results emerging from university science departments recently offer impressive proof of the existence and effectiveness of healing on humans, animals, plants, fungi, and cancer cells.

Colors, which are specific wavelengths on the electromagnetic energy spectrum, are an effective vibrational healing energy, as is the harmonious

sound energy that we call music or the voice of a loved one. In addition to the senses of sight and hearing, the rest of the five senses are stimulated through the nervous system in vibrational energy form, so that evocative perfumes, inviting textures, and delicious foods are equally health giving. In spring, we experience our world through our five senses very keenly after the coldness and darkness of winter.

How can you affect your own environment to enhance your well-being? What changes of colors, music, textures, perfumes, foods, and loving emotions can you use to transform your surroundings? Note in your Spirit Diary what you have decided to change for the better.

Loving connections

Wedding ceremonies and rituals evoke loving emotions, and this sacred information has a positive effect on the couple who are to marry, the congregation of wedding guests, and the place of celebration. The vibrations of love and happiness at a marriage are absorbed by the people and by the physical surroundings.

What do you see in them?

*   Think of the people whom you love. What is it that you love about them? What qualities do they possess? Have you ever specifically told them what you love about them? Tell them, or write them a note, or in some other creative way communicate your appreciation of their qualities. Note all their qualities.

What do you see in me?

*   Ask your friends what they value most about your friendship. Make a list of the things they tell you. Notice that what they admire, although they probably do not realize it, is also one of their own attributes. Reread the list of loved ones' qualities from the above exercise. Do you realize that you also have these qualities, otherwise you would not have been able to recognize them in others?

On love

This is a great way to reintroduce yourself to all your positive experiences about loving, so that with a refreshed, revitalized memory you become more aware of the power of love in your life.

* Imagine walking through a perfect pink cloud (we associate the color pink with love).

* Emerge from the color and find yourself sitting alone in a small, magic theater. The movie that is playing is a portrayal of the place that love has in your life. See your images of love projected onto the screen, and when the film is over, ask the angel projectionist to give you the cassette of film to keep safely in your heart.

* When you are ready, walk back through the colorful cloud, return to the here and now, and open your eyes.

Learning about love

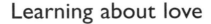

* Close your eyes and take three deep breaths, concentrating each time on the out breath.

* Review all the times in your life when you learned a positive lesson about love.

* Open your eyes and write down your most vivid loving memories in your Spirit Diary.

Flower essences

Flower essences, like homeopathy, are beautiful forms of vibrational energy treatment and can be found in most good health food stores. Discover which flower essences contain the energy of love, relationships, and commitment. Remind yourself of the vibrational energy quality of love and add this knowledge of the help that these remedies can give to your resource. Take them if or when you feel the need for them, or recommend them to loved ones.

ILLUMINATING

The second quarter of our journey is a time for being present, setting and achieving goals, and enjoying life. It is a time for us to pause in our spiritual journey to ask which path forward we should now choose. In the wise words of the ancient Chinese sage Confucius, "Every great journey is made of small steps."

Azure skies appear overhead, the sunshine warms us, and we venture forth to find our place in the sun. As our energy and influence expands in the summer heat, we permit ourselves to relinquish old, limiting ideas that imprisoned us and prevented us from realizing our true potential.

Turquoise seas, the sounds of the amusement park and seabirds flying overhead, the feel of fine silver sand between toes—all these sensations help us to recall harmonious childhood holidays. Harmony is an important aspect of this season, and the Eastern disciplines of *I Ching*, Feng Shui, and Nine Ki bear direct relation to this.

Summer's warmth pervades our lives, filling us with appreciation. As we focus on good deeds and noble intentions, our souls are enriched by the purity of these spiritual activities and emotions. We reflect on love and the fundamental quality of the energy of the universe.

MONTH

4

Asking advice from the Spirit World

Divination

To thine own self be true

The power of self-knowledge

Clear the clutter

The flow of lovingkindness

Joy and laughter

Asking advice from the Spirit World

Your soul's energy has emerged into the world, but before you continue on your spiritual journey it is useful to consult a wise friend on which path to take next. When you allow yourself an awareness of the existence of the wisest of friends of all—the guides, ancestors, and celestial beings in the realms of the Spirit World—it becomes natural to connect with them and ask for their advice. What these beings are is the sum of the love, energy, and wisdom of the departed souls who still care for us and wish us well. They live on eternally as faithful messengers of Spirit, as do those celestial beings that have never manifested physically in our world—the angels, cherubs, and seraphs that bring powerful healing, blessings, and loving energy to enrich our lives.

Divination

Divination techniques allow us to invite the voices in Spirit to advise us about the future. They are best used to ask for advice about our spiritual development. There are many methods of divination available for obtaining spiritual advice, including the *I Ching*, the Tibetan Mo Oracle, the runes, Celtic wisdom sticks, angel cards, tarot cards, and tea leaf readings. Divination requires us to meditate until we feel confident of the connection with Spirit and then to consult the oracle in the ways prescribed for each individual method (coins, cards, sticks, stones, tea leaves, or pages of a book).

When I am meditating on profound spiritual issues, I prefer the wisdom of the *I Ching*, the ancient Chinese *Book of Changes*, in one or more of its many translations; the amazing imagery of the tarot also relates strongly to the psychic and mediumistic aspects of the mind. When, however, I need good straightforward comment on a practical course of action, I consult the Tibetan Mo. For instance, when deciding whether to write this book, I asked the Mo Oracle, which replied:

Listen, O Inquirer!

This matter requires the bold advance of a lion; act like the lord of lions! If you proceed in that way, there will be no need for fear. Your protecting deity is very powerful, so you will succeed. Just as honey can be taken when the bees have been cleared away, act in reliance on yourself, and you will definitely succeed.

To thine own self be true

The hectic growing period at the start of our journey yields its place to a maturing phase during which we begin to understand who we are and what we can achieve in life. The warmth and fullness of this season, the feelings of easy living that the strong sunshine encourages, offer us the opportunity to pause and reflect on our own inner nature. William Shakespeare, in his play *Hamlet,* wrote, "This above all: to thine own self be true, / And it must follow, as the night the day, / Thou canst not then be false to any man."

Be the Lion

Sometimes, with the best of intentions, we find that we have allowed limitations to be imposed on our progress. Our own authentic voice becomes muted as we absorb the constraints of our community's expectations and we prevent ourselves from assuming our place in the sun. The following southern African traditional story illustrates this.

Once upon a time, a lioness gave birth to a perfect cub. She marveled at her creation and felt complete love for her small son. She realized that she had to feed him so she hid him in a safe place and set off in search of prey. Soon after she left him,

a terrible storm tore through the skies. The mighty thunder, the hard, driving rain, and the howling wind made the tiny lion cub extremely frightened; he felt abandoned by the soft, loving presence that he had called "Mother."

He did not know what she looked like because his eyes had not yet opened, but he thought he would only be safe if he could find her again. So he stumbled out into the wide world to search for her, until he was exhausted, terrified, and desolate.

As the storm ended, he fell down in a meadow and cried piteously. There was a flock of sheep in that meadow and a compassionate ewe, who had given birth to many lambs, trotted over to the cub and, licking away the tears from his opening eyes, asked him what was the matter.

"I want my mother!" he sobbed.

"I am not your mother, but would you like me to look after you?" asked the ewe as she gently nuzzled him.

"Oh, yes please!" cried the lion cub.

And so it was that the lion grew up with the flock of sheep until one day, a year later, the lioness—who had been searching ceaselessly for her lost cub—came upon a curious sight. There in a meadow was her son, now an adult lion with a glorious mane, grazing happily and surrounded by sheep.

She bounded up to him, licked him joyfully, and said,

"My darling son, at last! And what a magnificent lion you have become!"

The lion recoiled from her in fear and replied, "No! I am not a lion! I am a sheep!"

"You are a lion. Be the lion you are! Speak with the voice of the lion!" commanded the lioness.

"Baa-baa-baaaaaa!" bleated the lion.

The lioness led her son to the edge of a lake. As he stood next to her, she told him to look down into the water. "That is your reflection," she said. "Reflect on your true identity."

He reflected on his true identity, and he roared with the voice of the lion.

The power of self-knowledge

Often society's norms have been offered to you with love and care to teach you how to be acceptable to the community group. Although it is important to respect the sincerely held beliefs of others, the awareness of self-knowledge releases you from the views of society that do not empower you. When you become certain of who you truly are, you can be present in the world with confidence. The way you see yourself is the main determining factor of the way others will perceive you. If you enter a room feeling that you are not worthy of being noticed, people will often behave as if you were invisible. People who enter a room feeling confident project energy, causing others to turn around and acknowledge their entrance.

A friend of the late Marilyn Monroe told how, one summer's day, she and Marilyn were walking in Manhattan, talking earnestly about a subject on which they both felt strongly. Marilyn was wearing no makeup, a head scarf, and a plain coat, and nobody noticed the famous film star. As they came to the end of their conversation, Marilyn whispered to her friend, "Shall I be HER now?" Immediately she was recognized and mobbed, causing traffic chaos. Her friend says the amazing thing was that she did not seem to change anything outwardly, she just decided to think of herself differently—and the effect was incredible.

When you believe in yourself, you alter the information in your aura and give different messages out to the universe. This is because each thought is a unit of spiritual energy. When you have positive thoughts about yourself you invest positive energy into your aura. Along with many people attending a seminar by the American authority on the psychology of peak performance, Anthony Robbins, I entered a hypnotic state—free from the negative emotional clutter of doubts and fears—that enabled me to walk on coals burning at a temperature that melts steel, and was completely unharmed. My fire walk convinced me that we are capable of extraordinary feats when we free ourselves from negativity. Do not go jumping out of windows thinking you can achieve flight on the strength of this idea, but set positive goals and go all out to achieve them!

Clear the clutter

Just as it is useful to clear the negativity that stops us from fulfilling our dreams, it is helpful to clear the clutter from our physical environment. Amazingly, when we change something on a physical plane we also seem to change it in the spiritual dimension.

A tidy space in which to live and work is one of the first principles of the ancient Chinese art of placement known as Feng Shui (which translates as Wind, Water and refers to an appreciation of the energy of natural elements). Many people in the West have developed an interest in Feng Shui. Those who use it wisely endeavor to create a dynamic spiritual harmony in their lives rather than to manifest a quick fix of money, romance, or success.

Feng Shui was developed to select fitting burial sites for the ancestors, but from this study of earth energies and landscape configurations grew an understanding of the effect of internal landscapes of the physical homes in which people lived. The first home of a person's soul is the body. The second home is the house, then the workplace. When a Feng Shui practitioner makes recommendations and creates a sacred space that heals the dwelling places and working environment, energy is made available to the dwellers for their health and well-being.

Honored guest

It is rare for us to observe our homes on a spiritual level, and so difficult to make changes that promote a more positive spiritual environment. This visualization helps you realize what needs to be done to begin to allow optimal auspicious energy—or as the Chinese call it, *ch'i*—to flow into your home and into your life.

✳ Imagine that you are an honored guest who is visiting the place where you live for the first time. Stand at the gate and view the property. Imagine what kind of person might live here. Is there any alteration, repair, or decoration needed? Is the pathway straight or gently curved? Are there obstacles in the way? What does the entrance look like?

✳ Entering through the door, stand on the threshold and view the first area of the house. Is it welcoming to an honored guest? Is there any clutter to be cleared, any decorations or alterations to be done?

✳ Moving into the living room, repeat the process of assessment of clutter, alterations, and decorations before proceeding to visit the kitchen, dining room, bedrooms, study, library, bathroom, basement, loft, yard—whatever rooms and grounds make up your dwelling place.

✳ On opening your eyes, understand that you are an honored guest on this earth, and set about effecting any changes and improvements you have noticed in your visualization.

The flow of lovingkindness

Just as you have afforded yourself the respect due to you as an honored guest, so also must you know that you are able to invite others into your home and into your life. Sharing your life with a loved partner and/or family, friends, and colleagues is an opportunity to demonstrate the warmth of your lovingkindness. As summer is the season in which the warm climate encourages us to relax and spend a good deal of time outdoors, we come into contact more easily with others and we therefore have greater opportunities to touch each others' lives with lovingkindness.

Map of lovingkindness

This reinforces your awareness of the joy and satisfaction you have gained by being a generous soul.

* Draw a map showing the flow of lovingkindness in your life in relation to all the people you know and care about and the people you don't know but whose lives you have touched via your good and charitable deeds.

Joy and laughter

Kind thoughts and acts are a path to spiritual joy, an experience very accessible in this season. What is the place of joy in your life? Spend some time relaxing in the sunshine, reflecting on how you see joy and laughter in your life. It is said that laughter is the best medicine, and now we are discovering that it does indeed strengthen the immune system and guard against illness.

It is a sad fact that although children laugh around sixty times per day on average, adults laugh only a couple of times per day. What have we done to ourselves to stifle that laughter as we grow up? Research attitudes to laughter and joy by asking those who are closest to you—in your personal life and at work—what their views are on the subject. This will help you to understand more fully the influences on your own attitude to your right to bliss.

Happiness mantra

A mantra is a word or an image that assists us in meditation.

* Sitting comfortably, bring to mind a time when you were really happy because you had done something truly kind for another person or an animal.

* Create a visual image to represent this act of kindness and stay with it in your mind for a while. This is your happiness mantra. It is there for you whenever you feel the need to reconnect with this feeling of the spiritual joy of service.

MONTH

5

Beyond limiting beliefs

Sitting in the sunshine, relax and let your best ambition come to mind, the one that would do the greatest good for you and harm nobody. Write down all the limiting beliefs that have prevented you from realizing that ambition. Now turn every negative, limiting belief into a positive, enabling statement—for example, turn "I'll never amount to anything in this world" into "I'll easily and soon achieve my ambitions." Work out the steps to achieving your ambition and then *take them*.

The comfort of the known

Scientists once put a large number of baby rabbits in a cage in a corner of a large meadow, where they grew up able to see the world outside their cage but unable to run free. When the rabbits were a few months old, the scientists released them. Their cage had provided them with certainty and security. Now that it was open they were reluctant to leave it and explore the meadow and beyond. Their real prison was removed, but the prison in their minds remained.

The caged parrot syndrome

Sometimes, the context in which we live our lives creates barriers to our full understanding. Ask a child in North America to describe a parrot, and the likelihood is that the child will say, "The parrot is a brightly colored bird that lives in a small cage and learns to repeat what you say." Ask a South American child the same question, and that child's description will be of a brightly colored bird that flies in the rain forest and is wild and free. The North American child's answer is valid for her or his experience. As the bird has not been seen in its true habitat there is no way that the child can conceive of its natural existence. Although everyone's experience of life is in some way limited by cultural and family "realities," it is essential to remember that there is a cosmic reality of being that encompasses your own and many other truths, from which you can draw sustenance, support, and spiritual inspiration.

Creating harmony

In the West we seem to have caged up our spiritual insights and placed them under the general heading of religion, putting them into meeting houses that we visit a few times a year to pay lip service to a deity. If we really were to study the ideas underpinning the major world religions, we would find that the true importance of religious teaching is to guide us to an understanding of Spirit, to point the way to respecting all living things, and to experience the unconditional love that powers the universe. Nowadays, many people are rediscovering their spiritual nature by exploring not only Western culture but also Eastern concepts of harmony.

Ideas of the duality of energy, called yin and yang, are at the center of Eastern spiritual teachings about the universe. According to these philosophies, everything in the universe is made of varying proportions of yin and yang. Expansive, light, outgoing energy is described as yang, or masculine, energy and contrasts with the yielding, dark, containing yin, or feminine, energy. These differing kinds of energy are traditionally represented by a straight unbroken line for yang (▬▬▬) and two short lines for yin (▬ ▬). The heavens are totally yang, the earth is totally yin, wood is more yang than yin, water is more yin than yang.

The Turtle and the Universe

One legendary day, China's first ideal emperor and sage, Fu Hsi, was meditating by the River Luo, when he saw a turtle emerge from the water. Fu Hsi understood that much wisdom could be gained from observing nature, and so he studied the animal carefully. He realized that the turtle could symbolize the cosmos, with its domed shell representing the heavens and its base the earth. Moreover, Fu Hsi saw for the first time in the markings on this particular turtle's carapace the eight trigrams—symbols that consist of three horizontal lines, either solid (yang) or broken (yin)—that reflect how the world's opposing energies work in harmony with each other. Many centuries later the trigrams formed the basis of the I Ching.

The Bagua

Each of the eight trigrams attributed to Fu Hsi has been linked with a direction of the compass, a season, a time of day, a color, and to human characteristics such as strength, shyness, and calm. They also have specific numbers. Together they form the Bagua, a tool used to chart energy. Usually, the Bagua is represented in the form of an octagon, with a trigram on each side and a central area of harmony. Its numbers can be arranged in the Luoshu or Magic Square of Three, where the central number five symbolizes balance. Whichever way you add the numbers in the square—horizontally, vertically, or diagonally—the result is fifteen.

Midsummer is associated with the number nine and the explosive energy of the element of fire. The areas of one's life it represents are those of success, illumination, and outward acclaim. As balance is essential to maintain harmony, we must look at this time of the year to the opposite number on the Bagua, and its element, and pay special attention to those areas of our lives. The opposite number to nine is one, the element is water, and the life areas are work and career. Often, when outward fame and success are achieved, it's tempting to ease up and rest on one's laurels. The Bagua shows that this can destroy the harmony of our existence.

If you are attracted to this ancient Chinese wisdom you may find that the harmony you can create by harnessing the natural energy around you becomes a power pack from which to draw within your environment.

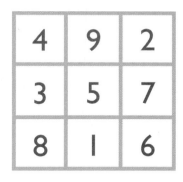

Diagram of Luoshu or Magic Square

The power of good intentions

The fifth month is a good time to continue studying the vast body of knowledge that is Feng Shui—a practice that will last a lifetime. By arranging your life in accordance with the forces of the universe you will achieve optimum health and prosperity. One of the first lessons to learn is that of the power of good and honorable intentions. A basic law of Spirit is that what you give, you receive. It therefore follows that focusing your good intentions on the well-being of others creates a positive energy that enhances your own existence.

The Poor Woman and the Feng Shui Master

A Feng Shui master was summoned by a distant prince to give expert advice on the positioning of a new palace. The journey was long and the summer sun was scorching. The master's horse needed a rest and he himself was parched, as he had not brought enough water with him. Eventually, in a valley just before his journey's end, he and his horse could travel no longer. The only building in the valley was a tumbledown shack. He approached and knocked on the door, which was opened by a poor woman in ragged clothes.

The woman was overwhelmed to find such a fine gentleman, wearing opulent silk brocade robes, at her door. She invited him into her shack to rest and recover, and she gave his horse some water in a nearby trough. To the master she offered her humble drinking bowl, filled with clear, cool, sweet, sparkling water. The master gratefully and hastily began to drink, but then the woman took a handful of chaff and threw it into the water, so that he had to drink very slowly and carefully in order to avoid swallowing the husks.

The master was very annoyed, and his anger increased as the old woman kept chattering to him, asking him questions that politeness bade him to answer and that slowed his drinking even more. In the conversation that ensued, she asked him how it was that such a grand gentleman was in her valley. When she learned his mission, she marveled that the prince had chosen this area to build his new palace. She told the master that she was a widow and her son, the only breadwinner, had just lost his job as a scribe. Now her family was destitute and in despair. She said that as her shack was on the point of falling down, it was necessary to rebuild it. As she was honored with the visit of such a knowledgeable master, could she please ask him to advise her where in the valley would it be most auspicious to rebuild it?

The master was furious that such a rude woman who threw chaff into a thirsty man's water could presume to ask for his valuable opinion, so he looked around until he found the most inauspicious place in the valley and pointed it out to her, saying, "That is where I advise you to build your shack!" Having managed finally to finish the bowl of water, he continued his journey.

Twenty years later, the prince decided to plan some extensions to the palace he had built, and once again summoned the Feng Shui master, causing him again to travel through the same valley. When he entered the valley, he was amazed to see a mansion set among beautiful gardens and surrounded by fields of thriving, luscious crops in what he considered to be a

most inauspicious position. He had forgotten about the poor woman in the shack, and his professional curiosity was aroused enough for him to stop his journey and find out who lived there. A servant answered the door and welcomed him inside. When the mistress of the house entered soon after, he suddenly recognized her and remembered what had happened twenty years before.

"Oh, Master!" she cried, "I bless you every day for the good advice you gave me! Since I rebuilt my shack here, all my crops have thrived and my son was given the post of chief chamberlain to the prince."

"So, you remember me," said the master.

"Certainly, and I also remember what a dehydrated state you were in that day! How quickly you wanted to gulp down the water! Why, so that you did not go into shock and die, I had to throw chaff into your water and slow down your drinking with idle chatter!"

The woman had saved the master's life by her hospitality, care, and good intentions, so the gods had intervened and overridden all the elemental laws of nature to grant her a good and blessed existence.

The four-heart sutra

This meditation is taught by the great ayurvedic practitioner Deepak Chopra, founder of the Chopra Center at La Costa Resort and Spa in Carlsbad, California. It comes from the ancient Indian holistic medical system of ayurveda. According to this body of understanding, we can open the center of our being—allowing good energy to flow through us—by simply imagining the heart physically opening and magnifying good intentions for the benefit of all.

Ayurveda teaches the importance of being in tune with nature and of adapting diet and lifestyle with the seasons. Midsummer is a time full of expansive fiery energy, which can be harnessed to great effect. Emerald is the color through which we will access this meditation, since the energy of the heart center is associated with green light. Expanding your energy into infinity nourishes the soul and can be used to relieve the accumulated stresses of modern life.

* Sitting comfortably in the pharaoh position (see page 8), close your eyes and imagine walking through an emerald-green cloud, leaving all your thoughts behind. When the beautiful cloud clears and you instinctively know that you are in a very safe space, innocently turn your attention to your heart and be aware of its beating.

* Repeat each of these four sutras four times:

   Every part of my body has absorbed wonderful light. I direct all that light into my heart. Now that my heart glows full of light, I open my heart and let my light illuminate the universe.

   Every cell in my body has vibrated to the sound of my laughter. I collect the memory of all the times my whole body has shaken with laughter until I cried with mirth, and I fill my heart with all my laughter. Now that my heart is practically exploding with my laughter, I open my heart and let all my laughter resound around the universe.

   Within every atom of my body there is the pure sense of peace. I let the awareness of peace gather in my heart until my heart shimmers full of the energy of peace. I now open my heart and I give my perfect peace to the universe.

   At the center of my soul there is love. I let my love flow into my heart until my heart swells with the bliss of my love. Now that my heart overflows with complete love, I open my heart and tenderly give my love to the universe.

* You have given light, laughter, peace, and love to the universe and, as a child of the universe, so you have received light, laughter, peace, and love.

* Walk back through the emerald cloud when you are ready to do so, picking up the thoughts you left behind as you return to the here and now.

Love thyself

Nourishing ourselves with cosmic and unconditional love is a practice sadly lacking in our usual busy schedules. We may sometimes need to focus on truly accepting ourselves before we can easily and effortlessly feel able to share that quality of love with others. If we love ourselves truly, then we do not need to search for love through a series of superficial sexual encounters; nor do we have to seek comfort and security by amassing money and possessions. A person who knows love understands that it is to be found at the deepest level of the soul. Only with self-esteem can we appreciate the satisfaction of gratitude for and derive comfort from our physical experiences and worldly possessions. It follows then that self-love generates interpersonal love and leads on to the quality of altruistic, unconditional love and compassion, which, in turn, heightens our awareness of the cosmic power of spiritual love. If we believe that on this earth in the physical dimensions of matter, time, and space we were lovingly manifested by and are the holographic fragments of the universal mind of a creator, or god, then we see our life force to be a spark of that divinity. When we are aware of our capacity to give love, we are in direct and wonderful connection with the divine Spirit.

In our day-to-day activities we are bombarded with images of impossibly perfect people trying to sell us things. The message is that if we buy a particular shampoo, breakfast cereal, car, toy, or fizzy drink then by association we will become perfectly beautiful, slim, and a world-class athlete, have blissful relationships, a successful career, glamorous friends, and well-behaved, attractive children. We may not be aware that shop mannequins are made so thin that, if they were real women they would be unable to menstruate; that there are billions of women who do not look like supermodels and only about eight who do; that Marilyn Monroe—one of the twentieth-century's most powerful sexual icons—was a voluptuous woman with a full and curvaceous figure; and that the average woman weighs 144 pounds (66 kg). Twenty years ago, models weighed 8 percent less than the average woman. Today they weigh 23 percent less. No wonder, then, that a psychological study in 1995 found that spending three minutes looking at a fashion magazine caused 70 percent of women to feel depressed, guilty, and shameful. We need to reclaim our delight in and respect for ourselves.

For the self

The following ritual teaches us to accept, appreciate, and love ourselves. This in turn enhances our capacity to give love to others without needing anything in return. If we cannot recognize feelings of love within ourselves, then we have no template with which to recognize the objects of our love outside ourselves. As without, so within; as below, so above.

* You will need a securely balanced bowl of water, out of the reach of children or household pets, and a supply of floating candles.

* On the first evening, pause after you undress for bed and before you put on your nightclothes. Take this moment quietly and peacefully to stand naked in front of a full-length mirror and notice just one small detail that you can accept, appreciate, and admire about your body. As a ritual gesture to celebrate this moment, light a floating candle in the bowl of water.

* On the second evening, quietly and peacefully stand in front of the mirror and, remembering the detail you have already noticed, look for another detail that you can also accept, appreciate, and admire about your body. Light a candle as before.

*   Repeat the exercise on the third evening and every evening after that until you have acknowledged and valued every tiny detail of your physical self.

*   When you have accomplished this task, devote the same amount of time and perception to recognizing aspects of your personality as well, each time letting your lighting of a candle remind you of the great light from which you came and to which you shall eventually return. You will in this way become aware of and able to celebrate the abundant blessings and gifts that make you unique and at the same time connect you to all life.

*   Soon you find that you can effortlessly marvel in gratitude at how miraculously all human beings are made and how divinely formed you are in your uniqueness.

MONTH

6

Respecting the miracle of life

Sexuality as a celebration of Spirit

"Know thyself"

You, now

Chakras

The bodymind and soul

Harmonizing body, mind, and Spirit

Respecting the miracle of life

Legend has it that someone once gave Indra, the Vedic warrior-king of the gods, a small and modest flower. He accepted the gift but then, considering it to be of no consequence, thoughtlessly threw it away. Lakshmi, the worldly earth goddess who brings vitally needed rains, withdrew herself, causing the earth to shrivel, until Indra learned that he had carelessly undervalued one of the many precious gifts of nature. When Indra realized his thoughtlessness, he repented and Lakshmi returned, restoring life to the world as a token of her forgiveness.

Just as the tiniest, most seemingly insignificant wild flower is a manifestation of the beauty and diversity of the cosmic mind and therefore sacred, so are our bodies. As the ancient Chinese sage Lao-tzu, author of the *Tao Te Ching*, reflected, "He who loves the world as his body may be entrusted with the empire."

No two flowers grow alike, and no two bodies are alike—even identical twins have some individual distinguishing characteristics. It is therefore fitting that in this month we celebrate the physicality of the body and what it can achieve as a sacred gift from Spirit.

Sexuality as a celebration of Spirit

The Hindus have a saying: "There are many paths up to the same mountaintop." Theirs is a broad faith that can accommodate diverse cultural and philosophical strands—of renunciation, asceticism, and detachment on the one hand and of religio-cultural practices in which sex plays an important part on the other. The *Kama-Sutra*, written by the third-century Hindu sage Vatsyayana, is a sacred treatise on the art and science of ecstasy attainable through sexual practice. Hindu Tantra is a spiritual path that aims to find release through working with and transforming the whole of the body, mind, and emotions. It is largely known in the West for its use, under strictly controlled circumstances, of sexual intercourse as a meditative technique.

Built by the Chandella rulers from the tenth to twelfth centuries A.D., the temple sculptures at Khajuraho in India's Madhya Pradesh region help to clarify the role of sexuality in certain cultural and religious customs of Hinduism. The walls of the temples are carved with erotic images that are a symphony to ecstasy and pure joy. Mostly, they celebrate the supreme bliss to be attained by merging the male (Shiva) and female (Shakti) energies of the universe. The temple carvings also depict naked men and women exhibiting their genitalia (according to ancient magico-religious beliefs and practices, such exposure was effective in warding off evil) to ensure the availability of auspicious sexual energy.

116

The thirteenth-century Sufi poet Jalaluddin Rumi likens the love of Spirit to the love of a lover for his beloved:

Invoking Your name
Does not help me to see You.
I'm blinded by the light of Your face.
Longing for Your lips
Does not bring them any closer.
What veils You from me
Is my vision of You.

To the early Christian church sexuality was closely connected with sin. Women assumed the legacy of Eve as the instrument of sensual temptation, with the exception of Mary, the mother of Jesus, who remained a virgin. Sexual activity in marriage was promoted but was viewed as inferior to chastity. Sexual abstinence is still demanded of Christian monks and nuns as well as all Roman Catholic clergy. Such devout groups are not confined to Christianity, however, but can be found in most other belief systems. In Buddhist monasteries, for example, abandonment of attachment to the physical world is a prerequisite of spiritual enlightenment.

In Judaism we find attitudes to sexuality akin to Hindu attitudes of physical sensuality, sexual lovemaking between married partners being encouraged and celebrated as a mitzvah, or sacred good deed. Sacred good deeds are an important aspect of Jewish practice, since it is considered everyone's responsibility to offer good deeds to one's fellows. By the practice of good deeds, Jews hope to hasten the day when the world will be fit to receive the Messiah—whom some Jewish mystics, students of the Kabbalah, believe will be in the form of an era rather than necessarily one person.

"Know thyself"

There are many different paths to spiritual bliss. Some cultures place particular emphasis on fasting and prayer, others access ecstatic feelings through physical activity. In Ancient Greece, communities and individuals used to bring their dilemmas to the oracle at Delphi. The oracle was presided over by the god Apollo, and at the entrance of the cave there was famously carved "Know thyself." It is important for our health and well-being that we do know ourselves emotionally and physically as well as spiritually.

Who are you? What do you want?

In month four you embarked on a journey of self-knowledge
(see page 80). This exercise can take you more deeply into
an understanding of who you are, sometimes in very
surprising ways, and can be a fundamentally emotional
experience. You will need your Soul Friend to join you in this.

*   Ask your Soul Friend to sit comfortably with you and, every
    fifteen seconds, repeat the question, "Who are you?" Your Soul Friend must
    not react in any way to your answers but persistently ask the question for
    at least ten minutes. Repetition of the question in this way does not give
    you time to construct erudite replies as you otherwise might in normal
    conversation. You may find that after you have exhausted the familiar ideas
    of how you define yourself you arrive at some answers that amaze you in
    their profundity, and that you unearth a mine of hidden depths, talents, gifts,
    desires, and magical connections.

*   Now repeat the exercise, but this time your Soul Friend asks, again at
    fifteen-second intervals for at least ten minutes, "What do you want?" This
    gives you the opportunity to search deep into your hopes and dreams.

You, now

At this central point in the year, who you are and what you want are central to your life's journey in this world, and the clarity that this knowledge brings enables you to make important decisions at a spiritual level. Your clarity also has the advantage of helping others to be clear about who they are and what they can expect from you. It is like shining the light of your focused soul into the darkness of the world of uncertainty, illuminating the present moment. Again let us admire the poetic wisdom of Jalaluddin Rumi:

Do not look back, my friend.

No one knows how the world began.

Do not fear the future, nothing lasts forever.

If you dwell on the past or the future

You will miss the moment.

Your existence is in the present moment, with only memories of the past, stored learning and wisdom, and hopes for the future.

Chakras

In the Hindu tradition, every person has a subtle body, which houses the mind and the intellect, and a physical body. Chakras (from the Sanskrit word for wheel) are powerful energy centers that provide a bridging mechanism between the two bodies. The seven major and twenty-one minor chakras are described in Hindu sacred literature, in particular in the *Shri Jabala Darshana Upanishad*, the *Cudamini Upanishad*, the *Yoga-Shikka Upanishad*, and the *Shandilya Upanishad*.

Clairvoyant people can see chakras; clairsentient people can feel them as they spin on their positions on the body. Emotional or mental blockages and physical traumas imbalance and impede the chakras in their spinning motion, creating lack of ease, or disease. Spiritual healing and physical practices such as yoga help to maintain balance and clarity in these energy centers.

When Candace Pert mapped the sites of clusters of receptors in the body, she found that they corresponded to the positions of the chakras.

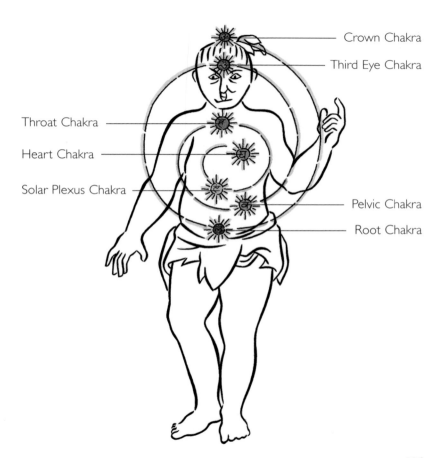

Crown Chakra

Third Eye Chakra

Throat Chakra

Heart Chakra

Solar Plexus Chakra

Pelvic Chakra

Root Chakra

The bodymind and soul

Since René Descartes announced in the seventeenth century that mind was entirely separate from matter, medical science has been able to explore the functions of the body as an entity in isolation—and doubtless many practical, lifesaving discoveries have followed from this belief. In the relatively young science of psychology, begun as a discipline in the nineteenth century, the importance of the body has often been ignored. Today, there are significant advances in our understanding of the relationships between the body, the mind, and the soul.

Candace Pert, a research professor at Georgetown University in Washington, D.C., was one of the first scientists to prove a connection between our physical and emotional selves. Lying in the hospital with a back injury, she was given morphine, which she realized was replacing her pain with a state of bliss. She reasoned that as we are able to reach blissful states, we must have a system for the production of internal, physiologically produced opiates that also function as painkillers. In 1973, she proved the existence of groups of ligand proteins called receptors in the walls of cell membranes all around the body. She reasoned that the function of these receptors must be to connect with the natural painkillers that our body must be producing. She further had the idea that the reactions between "messenger molecules" and their receptors could create vibrational impulses carrying health information to the cells. This opened up the opportunity for the opiate messenger molecules, endorphins, to be discovered by scientists in Aberdeen, Scotland. Soon the world of medical research established a new body of knowledge called psychoneuroimmunology—or bodymind medicine—charting the interconnectedness of the emotions, the mind, the nervous system, and the immune system.

Candace Pert has also demonstrated that the two emotions that have the greatest health-giving effects on the physical body are the very same that spiritual visionaries and leaders throughout all religions advocate: love and forgiveness.

Deepak Chopra, the celebrated endocrinologist, ayurvedic practitioner, and author, has also contributed significantly to our understanding of the bodymind and the soul. He trained as a doctor in his native land of India before traveling to the United States to practice medicine. Here, he became increasingly dissatisfied with a Western healthcare system that was obsessed with the absence of disease rather than the promotion of perfect health. He turned to his own cultural roots, to the study of ayurveda, the Indian mystic system of healing, and began to gather Western scientific data that illustrated its validity. Since then his mission has been "to bridge the technological miracles of the West with the wisdom of the East."

Bernie Siegel, an oncologist, realized through his work with cancer patients that those who were in love with life and were determined to continue living stood a far better chance of survival than those who did all the right things and took all the right treatment, out of fear of death. Their positive attitude and his acquaintance with Jungian therapeutic techniques and art therapy drew him to devise support groups for what he termed his exceptional cancer patients, known as ECaP Groups. He focused the attention of the mainstream medical world on the connection between the body and the mind, linked with clarity of Spirit, and with his warmth and humor gently opened minds that might have formerly remained closed to such ideas.

Harmonizing body, mind, and Spirit

The actor and public speaker F. M. Alexander, who invented the Alexander Technique at the beginning of the last century, used to tell his students, "When you allow the body to stop doing what is wrong, then it automatically does what is right." In your Spirit Diary, record what connections you are aware of between your physical, emotional, mental, and spiritual states, and what you are doing to harmonize them.

Journey into space

This meditation helps the mind to stop its constant chatter and sending of thoughts to the body. It is an effective way to achieve harmony and clarity. It is particularly useful when you have a worry that needs resolving.

✳ Sitting comfortably in the pharoah position (see page 8), spend a short time formulating a question about something that might be occupying your thoughts today.

✳ Imagine writing the question on a beautiful parchment paper in violet ink, as violet is the color with the highest vibration of the visible spectrum of light.

✳ In your mind, place the parchment in a special wooden box with hinges and a fastening of gold, leaving it in a very safe place where Spirit helpers can sense your question and eventually provide an answer.

✳ Come away from this place and feel yourself becoming lighter and lighter as you rise up, away from the world and into the indigo void of space. As the indigo surrounds you, focus your eyes on infinity and travel further into space until you reach a point of connection with the heart of the cosmos.

✳ Stay in this perfect state of being for as long as you feel comfortable before returning through space to the safe place where you retrieve the special wooden box. Open its golden fastening and find that the parchment on which your question was written has been replaced by another parchment on which has been written the answer, which you now read.

* Thank the Spirit helpers for their advice, smile, and return gently to the here and now.

GATHERING

The ripening fruits of our experiences are heavy on the vines, brambles, shrubs, and trees, and the plump grains of self-knowledge are golden and ready for harvest, testifying to the abundance of the universe. Our energy is gathering and downward in direction. There is an opulence about what we have learnt and our store of knowledge stands like the market stalls piled high with nuts, apples, pumpkins, pears, and much more.

As children play in piles of fallen leaves, the sounds of the outdoors quieten. Many birds are flying south, no longer adding their voices to the dawn chorus. People hurry to the warmth of their homes rather than linger in sidewalk cafés, parks, or gardens. There is an increasing urgency to prepare for the coming of winter and to make our homes welcoming and bright. Friendships that were casually kept in the relaxed days of summer now are nurtured with more formal invitations of hospitality. The love we have for friends is precious in so many ways, and giving it expression at the end of this season warms the heart up as the temperature outside cools down.

MONTH

7

The season of work

Taking pride in your work

Cooperative working

Reaping what you have sown

The season of work

When you think about the work you do, how do you feel? Enthusiastic? Ecstatic? Bored? Depressed? What happens when you are at work? What can you find in your habitual actions that you can turn into a spiritual celebration? In the United States the death rate for the week peaks at 9 A.M. on Monday mornings, a statistic that indicates how stressful negative attitudes to work can be. Being spiritually at peace with the work you are doing is vital to your health and well-being.

If you are aware that your health is being affected by your present job, then obviously it is important to weigh the status or the monetary rewards against the effect on you personally and, if necessary, ask yourself whether now would be a good time to start looking for a new job. Most people feel that it is not necessary to take such radical action, but realize they may need to acquire more positive attitudes to the work in which they are daily engaged.

Applying mindfulness

The Buddhist concept of mindfulness—constant awareness of the body, feelings, state of mind, and mental processes—can transform everyday routines into marvelous events. When carried out mindfully, you can even turn the semiautomatic actions of walking into a hymn to life.

* Standing still in one place, feel the way your feet adjust to the distribution of your weight and keep you in upright balance.

* Before you decide to lift a foot in preparation for your first step, imagine how it is going to feel and what changes the foot remaining on the ground will have to experience.

* Lifting your foot, experience the physical freedom that release from contact with the floor gives it and imagine how it is going to travel forward to its next position on the floor.

* Step forward, focusing your mind on every single state and change in your position and balance.

This technique teaches us to marvel at the amazing complexity of the body and the intricacies involved in accomplishing even the dullest of tasks. By applying mindfulness to your daily routine, you will gain an increased awareness of the complexity and satisfaction in the physical process of your work, become heartened, and therefore achieve more.

Taking pride in your work

C. G. Jung, one of the founding fathers of psychotherapy, studied a tribe of South American Indians who never suffered from the harmful effects of Western-style anxieties and stress. They experienced little illness and lived long, harmonious, and peaceful lives. They believed that the ritual prayers they conducted every morning enabled the sun to rise and give light, warmth, and life to the world, and that it was their responsibility to perform a similar ritual every evening to ensure the setting of the sun so that it could rest in preparation for its labors the next day.

It is not necessary to believe that the world's very existence depends on your doing your job, but do take time to consider the benefits your work brings to your community. If you do, the heightened enjoyment you experience will not only positively influence your self-esteem and pride in what you do but also set a shining example to your colleagues.

It is possible to develop a more positive attitude to a job and to form closer ties with colleagues, but if you are fundamentally unhappy at work then no amount of effort and compromise can salvage the situation. There are many reasons why people leave their jobs. Some have ethical misgivings about the end product; others sense that they will never have a satisfying relationship with their coworkers; most instinctively feel that it is time to move on. If in your heart you know the job you are doing is not for you, then it might be time to do some positive quitting.

The accelerated future mirror

This powerful exercise can help to sort out how you truly feel about your work.

* Sitting comfortably and quietly, surround yourself in a beautiful color. Imagine walking through the color into a safe place, where you sit down in front of a mirror. Look into the mirror and see yourself honestly reflected there, and see in the background what is happening in your work at the moment.

* Without making any decisions and without anything having changed at work, travel six months into the future and sit down at the mirror. What do you see happening at work, and what are you saying to your reflection in the mirror?

* Travel a year into the future and repeat the exercise, then two, five, ten, and twenty years into the future. What have those twenty years done to you? What is happening in your working life if you have not made any decision to change?

If you feel content to have left things exactly as they are, it is more than likely that you are in the right job at present. If this exercise left you screaming for mercy, then it is time to retire or to start reading the "Help Wanted" columns of the newspapers. Always be sure that you are going with the flow of your life force and not against it. Your energy is the stuff of your soul.

Make a list of all your skills, your morals, and your principles. How can you combine these and incorporate them into activities that are satisfying and meaningful to you, remembering that both street cleaners and rocket scientists are equally valuable within our communities?

Cooperative working

At work try using some simple techniques that are sure to aid communication. Neuro Linguistic Programming (NLP) gives us very useful skills in this domain. For example, when in a business meeting, seek eye contact and assume a posture that is the mirror image of the person you are talking to. This gives the impression that you are looking at someone who, if not actually yourself, is physically and therefore in all probability emotionally in tune with you. Listen carefully to the images and metaphors the other person uses in her or his speech and employ the same metaphors to illustrate your views. With high-quality communication comes connection, and with connection comes spiritual harmony. These NLP techniques are also very effective outside the workplace in social settings, where mirroring someone's posture is an easy way to put a person at ease.

Working together with other people can be very rewarding. "All of us is better than any of us." However, it can also be very stressful if the flow of ideas is impeded by disagreements and misunderstandings. Marianne Williamson, the celebrated metaphysician and author who teaches the world-renowned "A Course in Miracles", suggests that an effective approach to resolving disagreements is to ask, "What am I thinking about this person that God is not thinking?" "What is God thinking about this person that I am not thinking?" and finally "What am I not forgiving enough about?"

Stress reduction

This simple yogic breathing exercise can be used to reduce anxiety levels before entering a potentially stressful meeting.

* Sit comfortably and quietly after you have prepared your information for the meeting. Close your eyes and imagine yourself surrounded by a beautiful color. As the color clears, innocently focus your attention on your breathing, noticing how intelligent your body is. It knows how to breathe without your instruction. It can be trusted to take just the right size of breaths it needs.

* Now pay attention only to your out breaths and continue attending to these for a few minutes. This will help stimulate the network of nerves— the parasympathetic nervous system—that governs the relaxing, stress-reducing functions of our body, mind, and Spirit. This is in contrast to privileging the in breaths that, by stimulating the sympathetic nervous system, govern our fight, fright, and flight group of responses.

Reaping what you have sown

A French fable describes how the grasshopper, having sung all summer, found herself deprived when the cold winds started to blow. She went to her neighbor the ant, begging her for some food to tide her over until the good weather returned. The hardworking ant asked her what she had been doing in the hot weather, and she replied that she had been singing. Her neighbor was unimpressed and told her that now she should go and dance!

Not everyone, thank goodness, is as unkind as the ant. Neighborliness is a special sort of friendship and forgiveness is one of the major health-giving emotions. In the fall, we gather with our neighbors in seasonal ceremonies and rituals that draw us all closer together in the spirit of community cooperation so that we do not have to face the coming hardships alone. In the United States, Halloween is celebrated as an opportunity to frighten off malevolent Spirits by dressing up to become them, making jack-o'-lanterns to chase the dark shadows away, and trick-or-treating neighbors. Good-humored folk make sure they have lots of sweets and treats in store, ready to bribe their mischievous little visitors not to trick them. In Britain there is Guy Fawkes Day, with its bonfires, fireworks, baked potatoes, and parkin cake, when everyone gathers for parties to celebrate the survival of the Houses of Parliament from a seventeenth-century terrorist plot. In the north of the country, children celebrate Mischief Night by smearing molasses on doorknobs or knocking on doors and running away.

A great celebration at this time of the year in Britain is Harvest Festival, where in churches, schools, and village halls people bring the fruits of their crops to distribute to the needy of the community after giving thanks to God for the bounteous nature of the earth. In the United States, Thanksgiving is celebrated for many of the same reasons and with the same enthusiasm.

Harvesting your good deeds

This is an exercise to highlight what you have done to deserve the good things in your life.

* Sitting comfortably, begin to notice your breathing, focusing on the out breath.

* Allow your mind to review your present life situation. Identify some really good things in your life right at this moment and write them down.

* Now think back, retracing your steps until you are aware of everything you have done in the past to make these really good things happen.

On lovingkindness

Make a list of all the kind deeds you have done this month and all the times when you have been filled with compassion. Reflect in what way others have benefited from these. Reflect in what way you have benefited from these.

Mellow fruitfulness

In "To Autumn" the poet John Keats describes fall as the "Season of mists and mellow fruitfulness, / Close bosom friend of the maturing sun."

The following meditation is a beautiful way of appreciating the energy of fall and the fruits that you are ready to reap at this stage of your journey.

* Sitting comfortably, close your eyes, and feel yourself rise to a magical space high above you where you are given all the wonderful fruits of the fall harvest.

* Taking one fruit at a time, celebrate its color, texture, smell, and taste, each time offering up a little prayer to the Creator for all the fruits of the earth.

* When you have experienced the memories of all the fruits you can think of and offered thanks for each and every one, return to present consciousness and open your eyes.

MONTH

8

Emotional maturing

Nine Ki astrology

Being human

Positive reframing

Emotional maturing

In fall, the energy of harvest time affords us the opportunity for ripening and maturing. This is best accomplished if you have knowledge of your roots and beginnings and can take an overview of your journey along life's path to date. There is an old saying that the apple never falls far from the tree, meaning that although individuals separate from their parents to create their own life, usually stay within similar areas of behavior patterns. Often, women see themselves turning into their mothers and men into their fathers, no matter how hard they struggle to break the mold in the effort to be different.

Nine Ki astrology

Sometimes accepting and respecting a family member for who they are, not allowing who they are to constrain your unconditional spiritual love for them, helps to release you from old harmful patterns of hurting and being hurt. The Japanese system of astrology known as Nine Ki can be very helpful in shedding light on an individual's basic personality, the nature of their motivation in life, and their style of presenting themselves to the outside world. Ki is the Japanese word for *chi*, or energy of life, and the number nine refers to the areas of the Bagua (see pages 100/101). Ki astrologers also focus on an important aspect of Feng Shui known as the "Five Elements of Transformation," which teaches that all creation is thought to be divided into five elements: wood (representing plants, animals, people, and all living things), fire, earth, metal, and water. In the Bagua the numbers three and four are ascribed to the element of wood, the numbers six and seven are of the element of metal, and the numbers two, five, and eight are the earth group of elements. The fire element is nine and the water element is one.

When flowing harmoniously, wood feeds fire; fire creates earth (in the form of ash); earth when compressed creates metal; metal contains water and when hot metal cools, water is formed on its surface; water feeds wood. When combined stressfully, water destroys fire, metal chops wood, fire melts metal, water runs through earth, wood takes the nourishment out of the earth, and so on.

Depending on the year and month you were born, you have the vibration of one of the nine numbers of the Bagua, and therefore an aspect of one of the five transformational elements (plus two minor numbers) that influences your way of being in the world. By discovering which elements you and your family members belong to and are influenced by, you can begin to understand your and their basic natures in new and creative ways. For instance, a family member whose basic number vibrates in harmony with yours will construct an easy but not necessarily exciting relationship with you. A member whose number combines stressfully with yours produces a more passionate but potentially destructive relationship. The relationship can succeed if you both accept and allow for personality traits that you each possess, are basic to you, and cannot be changed.

Researching your family tree

When people study their family trees, generational patterns become easy to detect. Most families are filled with good and valuable traditions, which when realized can be lovingly and proudly cherished. Negative traits can also be spotted and discarded. Spend some time researching your family tree; draw it in your Spirit Diary, as the example below shows, with male family members represented by a square and females by a circle.

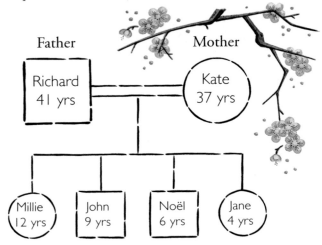

Father — Richard 41 yrs

Mother — Kate 37 yrs

Millie 12 yrs

John 9 yrs

Noël 6 yrs

Jane 4 yrs

Those who have died are indicated by an "x" through their symbol. The sign for "married to" is "=," "connected to" is "__." Those who are divorced are represented by "=/=," and the children of a marriage or partnership are shown as follows:

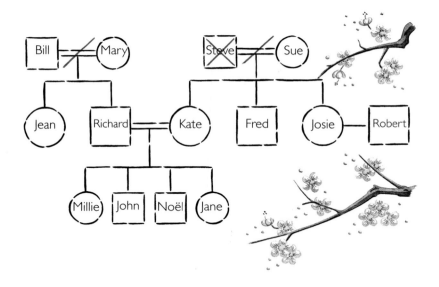

When you have constructed your own family tree, you may then find it useful to choose a color to represent strong positive feelings between two people, a second color to represent strong negative feelings between two people, and a third color to represent a very weak emotional link between two people.

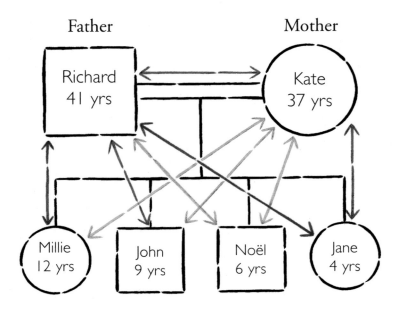

Now, examining your family tree, what patterns become clear? What can you deduce from these patterns? How have these traits affected you in your formative years and what principles of relating to others have you learned as a result of being born into this particular family? Show your family tree to your Soul Friend and see if the same patterns are clear to her or him. Ask your friend how her or his family is the same as or different from yours. Talk about what you value and want to keep of your family patterns, and what you would like to change for your life and for the future generations of your family. In this manner, you can become aware as an expert observer of your significant early emotional influences, you will be able—if necessary—to make liberating decisions about your future happiness, and you will have embarked on a profound process of healing your family.

Being human

Before finding information about your innermost nature and that of those closest to you in your life, it is important that you understand that you are perfectly acceptable as an imperfect human being. Rachel Naomi Remen attended a seminar by fellow therapist Carl Rogers on "Unconditional Positive Regard." At the start of the class, Rogers turned to the group and said that before he began he would let himself know that he was enough—not perfect, because that would not be enough, but that he was human, and that was enough.

This stunned Rachel Naomi Remen. It felt as if some old wound in her, some fear of not being good enough, had come to an end. She knew, inside herself, that what Rogers had said was absolutely true: she was not perfect, but she was enough.

If people constantly strive to be perfect, measuring themselves against their idea of others and finding themselves wanting, not noticing their own positive attributes, they do not give themselves the opportunity to realize that what they are is beautiful, too. Some competition can be healthy, because through it you find you can sometimes reach new heights of achievement. This is the competition engaged in by those who are confident of their value at the start.

Reflection

This simple exercise teaches you to get to know and accept your own face intimately. By doing this, you can then see yourself as a beautiful creation with the history of your life in your face, just as a ripening fruit represents the story of its parent tree.

* Take a hand mirror and sit somewhere very comfortable. Gaze at your face in the mirror until you begin to look through it and into your life, from the physical to the metaphysical.

* Repeat this process with each feature of your face individually: eyes, nose, mouth, forehead, cheeks, and chin. With each feature, look for evidence of a life well lived. Notice the lines created by laughter and those created by frowns. Notice the dark circles chronicling late nights and the texture and clarity of the skin. Regarding your face as a miraculous construction, reflect on how it has changed as you have lived your life.

* Now take the opportunity to look at the faces of those around you. When you observe them in the same searching way, everyone you see becomes beautiful because life itself is beautiful and clearly visible in people's faces.

Positive reframing

In fall, the fruits of our lives' events ripen. Some are perfect, but others have been distorted by traumas along the way. A person who is affected by a shock in their life finds it difficult to see the present in a positive light. When we work with spiritual energy, we can take people into their pasts and enable them to rewrite their stories. The people in the following examples were able to move on happily once they could positively reframe their traumatic histories.

Simone is a young woman who has a high-powered and highly paid job that she loves. Nevertheless, for many years she felt depressed and, although her employers reassured her, was convinced that she was not secure in her work. I asked her to travel back to the first time she was aware of feeling these negative emotions, and she pinpointed a time about six years ago when she was working in Rome. She had been on a fixed-term contract but had done so well during the time she was working with the company that she was sure they would ask her to stay. She was shocked when her contract was not renewed and she suffered feelings of anger, depression, insecurity, and self-doubt. I asked her what happened as a result of having to leave that job. She replied that she had come to London, a city that she loved, and had landed her present job, which was much better. She was able to realize that instead of being a tragedy, losing the first job was in fact a lucky break. She eventually wanted to thank the people in Rome for not renewing her contract!

Her negative feelings have now disappeared and are replaced with feelings of security, gratitude, and contentment.

The second story is about a man who came to me because he was feeling tired all the time. When I was giving him healing I saw the Spirit of a horse and described her to him in detail. He identified her as his very first pony, and remembered how he loved her, and she him. Before he bought her, she had had a sad life, having been ill-treated by her previous owner. She was a gentle and passionately loving animal and under his tender care she recovered her trust in humans. One fateful day, they were out riding and his pony was straining to gallop so he took her into a meadow and gave her full rein. The day was sunny and everything in the world seemed perfect. It was then that his beloved pony had a heart attack and instantly died under him. He felt grief-stricken and guilty that he had not taken greater care of her, and from that day he became very depressed and tired.

I was able to suggest to him that he had given his pony a beautiful life and had earned her love and trust. How would she have chosen to die, if she had a choice? Galloping with her beloved human on a fabulous summer's day, of course! Not only had he given her a beautiful life, but also a perfect death. From that realization, he began to recover his strength and resolve his grief for his lovely little pony.

The colors of maturity

In this phase we are nourished by the ripeness and abundance of our journey's produce as it has grown to maturity for our harvesting. This simple color meditation gives us the opportunity to be on sympathetic wavelengths and at peace with our autumnal surroundings.

* Sitting comfortably in the pharaoh position (see page 8), imagine walking through a beautiful iridescent bronze color. Allow yourself time to bathe in this color from head to toe. Notice the many colors that make up the bronze: the shades of red, orange, brown, russet, copper, and gold. Take each color in turn and swirl it round your body, absorbing its warmth and magical richness.

* Now take a perfect white, the Feng Shui color of metal, and wrap yourself in its shimmering purity. According to the ancient Chinese masters, metal contains the energy of gathering and so is the element of fall. Wrapped in this brilliant fall energy, gently return to the full consciousness of the here and now, open your eyes, stretch like a cat, and smile a contented smile.

MONTH

9

Friendship

Reviewing your goals

Nutrition and health

The importance of love, hope, and
compassion

Prayers as medicine

Friendship

Fall crops are gathered, and we gather together also in friendship. There is something very comforting about the feeling of connection that friendship brings, so it is a good time of year to think about these special people and what they mean to you.

Who are your friends and how important are they to you? What kind of friend are you? Do you enjoy spending time with your friends when they are in need of support or are you one of the fairweather variety? Do you have time to listen to their troubles or do you prefer just telling them about yours? Can they share their pride in their achievements with you, knowing that you will be as thrilled by their successes as they are, or does the acclaim received by them only engender envy or the need for serious competition in you? Do you have enough friends or would you like to make more? What does being a good friend mean to you?

Use the answers to these questions to assess the state of your friendships and to decide what, if anything, you wish to change. Remembering that what goes around comes around, the privilege of giving support to a friend also sustains you, in that the love you offer your friend feeds back into your soul's aura and out into the universe.

Have you found yourself resenting the time spent buoying up sinking friends? Sometimes when two people have learned all that they can teach

172

each other, it is time to say good-bye and move on. It can be difficult, however, to let go if you think of yourself first and foremost as a loyal person. Remember, any self-definition is limiting. Knowing that you have chosen to be their friend, you are free to choose either to leave or to be enriched by your mindful service.

Appreciating your friends

This exercise confirms the value you place in the friends that you have. The second part of the task gives your friends an idea of their importance in your life.

* In your Spirit Diary, make a list of all the people who are your friends, not necessarily in the order of closeness. Beside each name, write down what you admire and value about this friend.

* Phone, e-mail, fax, or write to each friend, explaining about this exercise and tell them what you have written beside his or her name. You will find that your friends will usually receive this information with delight and might even reflect back to you just what it is that they appreciate about you, too.

Seeing the way ahead

The blind spot is an amazing visual phenomenon that can be used as a metaphor for the times in your life when you think there is no way through a seemingly intractable situation.

* Holding up this book in your right hand, with your right arm straight out in front of you, close your left eye and focus on the black dot in the diagram on the right.

* Very slowly bring the book closer to your right eye, all the time focusing on the dot until you reach a position where the gate disappears. This is the position we call the blind spot and with the book in this position we can be forgiven for thinking that the door does not now exist.

There are times in life when you may feel that you cannot see a solution to a problem and that probably a solution does not even exist. At that time remember that you may simply be looking from the position of your spiritual blind spot, and that perhaps if you adjust the focal length of your attitude to the universe, a solution can become clear. The gate to the way forward appears and you can choose to take it and continue on your path. Similarly, when you feel you have reached a metaphoric blank wall in your life, think yourself around the problem from all angles by adjusting your attitude rather than banging your head against it.

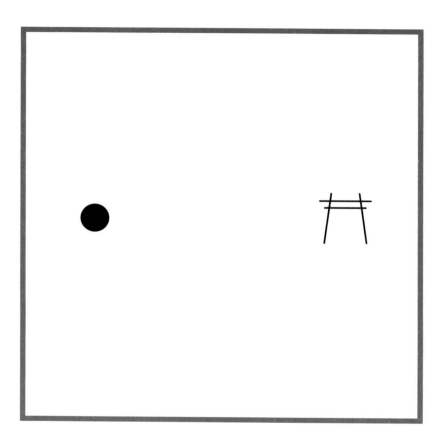

Circulating abundance

This exercise uses the energy of abundance and is based on the spiritual law "What you give, you receive." It aims to increase your awareness of the part you play in the lives of others and how by your actions you have the power to alter their lives for the better.

* Sitting in a peaceful place, gather in your mind all the reasons you have to be grateful for the good things in your life. Not everyone may be financially wealthy, but emotionally and spiritually you can certainly find a few reasons to celebrate the gifts you have been given: the gift of life, for instance, or of a beautiful day, of good friends, of a loving family, of a roof over your head, of a fulfilling job, of good health, and so on.

* With these personal blessings in mind, decide what you can do to share this feeling of abundance with others. You may feel that you want to contribute some money to a charity or volunteer your services in your spare time to help people or animals in need. Another way is to decide to befriend an old person living alone or in a retirement home, and make regular visits. Tell your Soul Friend what you have chosen to do and why.

Reviewing your goals

At the start of this book you did an exercise to establish your goals for the year (see page 23). How are you progressing? Are you on target? In your Spirit Diary draw a horizontal line across a page, marking the left-hand starting point as the beginning of Month 1 and the right-hand finishing point as the end of Month 12. Now distribute your goals as you have achieved them along the line and add any extra high points that helped your spiritual progress or setbacks that you needed to overcome. What do you still need to accomplish in the next three months?

Nutrition and health

With the emphasis at this stage of your journey being on gathering in your harvest, it is useful to think in general terms about the importance of the food you eat. These days the newspapers are constantly relaying a catalog of calamities involving the foods that are found to give you cancer or some other life-threatening condition. It stands to reason that a balanced diet gives you the building blocks for a healthy body, and a preference for organically grown food pays dividends in terms of your well-being. Add to this the idea that food energy and color are intrinsically linked. I remember twenty years ago being in the hospital and, after having major surgery, being given a meal of gray, steamed fish, gray, lumpy mashed potatoes, and gray, overcooked cauliflower. I felt immediately depressed! How was I going to survive and recover my health on such a diet? Luckily, my husband brought me wonderful fruit and tasty, colorful, nourishing savory treats that he and our friends had prepared, and raised my mood and my energy levels.

Remembering the ideas of balance and harmony, a meal should include various different textures and tastes. Food containing yin, or feminine energy, is by nature soft, like soups and purees. Yang foods are those with a bite, such as salads and raw fruits. Yin and yang is independent of the ingredients—a slice of bread is yin and the same bread toasted is yang. Ayurvedic tradition classifies food into six different categories—sweet, sour, bitter, pungent, salty, and astringent—and advises that a good, balanced meal contain all these tastes.

Gathering and giving

This meditation is designed to give you a great feeling of refreshment in a way that is as natural as breathing.

* Sitting comfortably in the pharaoh position (see page 8), close your eyes and imagine walking through a white cloud, since white has gathered into itself all the colors of the visual spectrum.

* Bring to mind one good thing that you have in your life. Gather the essence of it into your heart and then offer it up so that the universe can multiply it and share it with everyone.

* Bring to mind another good thing and another, until you can think no further. Each time offer it to the universe to multiply and share.

* Now think of some good things that you would like to be given. Let the universe know that you are now ready to receive them in abundance.

The importance of love, hope, and compassion

Physical health not only relies on good nutrition but also on spiritual connectedness by means of positive emotions. Married men statistically live longer, healthier lives than bachelors. Laboratory animals that are treated with love and compassion, and whose caregivers hope for their survival, last longer than those who are simply given food and water. Love, compassion, and hope can make a real difference to a person's survival. Is there someone in your life who is in need of your care right now? If there is, know that your spiritual connection with them at this time is actually beneficial on a practical level as well as an emotional one.

Prayers as medicine

Prayers have also been proved to have an amazing effect. In 1988 a scientist called Randolph C. Byrd and his colleagues in the University of California studied the power of prayer. A group of born-again Christians held prayer meetings lasting twenty minutes on a daily basis in a house three miles from the Coronary Care Unit (CCU) of the San Francisco Medical Center of the university. The first four hundred cardiac patients to be admitted during the research were randomly divided into the control group (around two hundred), who received the usual medical care, but for whom nothing extra was done, and the experimental group (around two hundred), who were given the usual medical care and whose names, ages, and individual condition on admittance to the CCU, with regular updates, were given to the prayer group. Members of the prayer meeting never met the patients, but prayed for all those whose names they were given.

When the results were analyzed it was found that the experimental group, for whom prayers had been said, had "10,000–1 against chance" better results of recovery than the control group, who had simply received the usual medical attention.

Please remember all those (including yourself) who may be in need of your love, compassion, forgiveness, hope, and prayers and give these emotions freely.

NOURISHING

As we approach the end of our year's spiritual journey we look within ourselves and take stock of our achievements and our progress along the path of knowledge. We prepare ourselves for the recommencement of the cycle of life and further continuation of our unique journey. At this stage of the life cycle, as in the winter season, we gather together with friends and lovers on long, dark evenings to warm and nourish ourselves in the glow of love and companionship.

In winter, the earth prepares for the creative demands of spring. Animals hibernate, renewing themselves for the year ahead; plants, seemingly killed off by the cold, nurture their roots in the hard soil. Remembering the warm sunshine, we realize that all hardships pass in time, and that an ending will always precede a new beginning.

Now is the time to refresh your soul. You have a life to lead that is unique. Consider now what contribution you can make to the world as you emerge from the darkness and into the light and hope that each new year brings. What power for the good do you possess that you alone can bring to this world? From your position on your unique life's path, how can you reach out to your fellows and really make a positive difference?

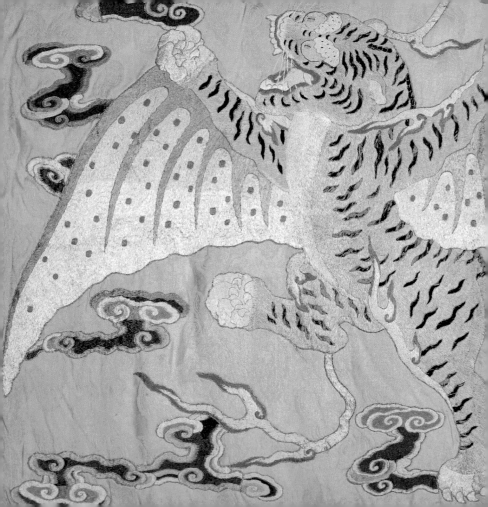

MONTH

10

Resting

Now is a time for rest and recovery. It is a natural process, so go with the cycle of the seasons, hole up, and enjoy the fruits of your harvest while dreaming of spring and all the new things you want to discover and achieve. Note in your Spirit Diary improvements you hope to make to your life when you have focused on the inner nourishment of your soul.

The icy winter weather can leave the earth's surface looking barren and forlorn, but the blueprints for new life lie buried deep in the ground waiting for the spring sun to warm the soil. Birds that remain with us over winter find it difficult to catch grubs to eat and rely heavily on the crumbs and birdseed left out for them. Nourishment is one of the keys to this stage of your journey, since we have stored up sustaining resources especially for this moment of the year.

If we did not experience cold, dark winter days, we would not appreciate the sun when it shines. There is no use protesting about the discomfort that inevitably comes our way this season, so why not concentrate on all the good things the harsh weather brings? This is the time when we begin to withdraw further into our homes, to our families, giving ourselves the opportunity to rediscover the love that we might find there.

As you may remember from Month 1's story about the wise farmer and the wild horse (see page 24), adverse conditions are not always what they

192

seem. Everything depends on the meaning with which you choose to invest them. Indeed, a cold, rainy day can be seen as a perfect chance to make a new friend, as an amorous Fred Astaire sang to Ginger Rogers in the 1935 film *Top Hat*:

I can see the sun up high
Though we're caught in the storm.
I can see where you and I
Could be cozy and warm.

Let the rain pitter-patter,
But it really doesn't matter
If the skies are gray;
Long as I can be with you,
It's a lovely day.

The wonder of dreams

Some animals hibernate in the winter season, entering into a long, deep sleep in dark and protected places, to emerge refreshed when the first touch of spring softness returns. When we humans sleep, we usually dream. We venture free and unfettered into an extraordinary world in which anything can seem to happen. Many great minds, and some not so great, have thought about the nature and the meaning of dreams. Aborigines, the indigenous people of Australia, refer to our everyday, fully conscious waking state as "The Dreamtime," believing that this "earthwalk"—or physical existence—is simply a lighter form of dreaming and that we have another more fully conscious awareness available to us, that being the true life of the soul. Sigmund Freud, the Viennese medical doctor who is widely held to be the founder of "the talking cure" of analytic psychotherapy, saw dreams in terms of coded messages to ourselves, which when translated and analyzed expressed our deepest repressed desires and preoccupations. Some think that dreams are a catharsis of unwanted thoughts, feelings, and sensations from our waking day. Others wonder if dreams are messages predicting the future or a means of taking us to the Spirit World.

The ancient Chinese sage Lao-tzu was famously known to ponder on the relationship between dreams and normal consciousness. He once awoke from sleeping, having dreamed that he was a butterfly. Awake, he wondered if he was a butterfly dreaming he was Lao-tzu.

Getting to know your dreamworld

Some dreams are unusually vivid and have a certain feel to them that disturbs or excites the dreamer into the idea that they are significant and should be acted upon. What if you were to dream of an impending calamity and did not take any steps of warning or protection as a result? When these dreams occur, tell a friend, write them down, and—if they will cause no harm—act upon them in as wise a way as you know how. They may or may not be delivered by heavenly messengers, but at the very least you will have peace of mind.

Get to know your dreamworld—it is about one-third of your life. Listen to what you tell yourself in your dreams. Explore your own symbolism and think of your dreamworld, which you visit every night, as a magical place, your own stage on which luscious, creative plays are unfolding.

Whatever the nature of your dreams, you might find it useful to record them, either in your Spirit Diary or a special notebook especially set aside for your dreams and your interpretations or ideas about them. Reflect on the bliss of your inner life and love, on the nourishing and restorative nature of sleep, and on the richness of your dreams.

Diffusing nightmares

Dreams are not always pleasant. Nightmares, by definition are frightening, and the terror that you experience in your dream world can remain to cloud your day. This exercise is to counterbalance and transmute nightmares into harmless and positively enjoyable daydreams. You will need a supply of paper and paints.

* On waking from a dream that has had the power to disturb you, paint a representation of the scariest moment of your dream. Call this Frame 1.

* Think of something wonderful that you really want to happen in your life, and paint the most ecstatic moment of this daydream. Call this Frame 4.

* Compare the two paintings, and design and then paint the missing frames 2 and 3 to link the two, so that in the end you have a four-frame series of paintings that transform your nightmare into the most beautiful experience you can imagine.

Another way to handle nightmares if they are of the recurring variety is to rehearse in your waking hours a point in the action where you will remember that this is only a dream. This takes some practice but eventually can be achieved, to dramatic effect.

The Huston treatment

Life's greatest certainty is that things will change. The lessons we learn from our experiences nourish our soul. To understand the future, you may need to reinterpret some of your understandings of the past.

Many years ago, I watched a television interview of the late film director John Huston. After the young interviewer had spent some time asking him about his impressive list of films—including *The African Queen* with Humphrey Bogart and Katharine Hepburn—he asked his big question, obviously designed to make an impact on the Great Man.

"Tell me, Mr. Huston," he said. "How is it that a man who is so clearly at the pinnacle of his chosen profession can be at the same time so patently unsuccessful in his private life?" He allowed himself the smile of the hunter when he is certain that his quarry is within his grasp. Huston asked him, in his slow drawl, what exactly he meant by that question.

"Well, you have had five unsuccessful marriages to date!"

"On the contrary, young man," responded Huston, "I consider three of those marriages to have been very successful!"

Applying this to your own life, search your past for a time that you classified as unsuccessful and give it the Huston treatment.

Chinese ideas about energy

Practitioners of traditional Chinese medicine call our life force, or vital energy, *ch'i* or *qi*. They teach that *ch'i* is channeled around the body in pathways known as meridians. For a person to stay healthy, an abundant supply of energy must flow through all the meridians. This can be aided through good diet and physical and mental exercises. The ancient Chinese discipline of Qigong uses movement, meditation, and visualizations to regulate the flow of vital energy through the meridians, thereby increasing physical and emotional energy and refreshing the soul.

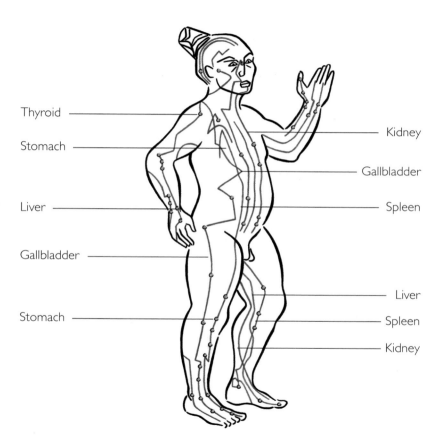

Thyroid

Stomach

Liver

Gallbladder

Stomach

Kidney

Gallbladder

Spleen

Liver

Spleen

Kidney

201

Qigong for soul refreshment

The Chinese discipline of Qigong is designed to increase your energy and refresh your soul. Thought is a form of spiritual energy and can be harnessed to enhance physical and emotional energy also. This basic Qigong exercise will give you a much-needed boost in winter.

* Stand with your legs slightly apart, your feet directly under each hip. Slightly bend your knees by curving your pelvis forward and tuck in your chin so that your spine is as straight as possible. Put the tip of your tongue into the roof of your mouth so that the underside is just touching the top of your mouth cavity, forming a connecting circuit of the energy meridians (see page 201) that run along these areas. Fold your hands flat over the center of your lower abdomen, and close your eyes.

* Taking slow, relaxed breaths, begin to direct the energy of a smile to play around inside your mouth but not on your lips. Increase the strength of the internal smile by spinning it until it becomes a powerful vortex of energy.

* When this energy is glowing very brightly, move it up from your mouth to a central point in your brain, about an inch behind your forehead. Let the energy blaze here, too, and spinning it further, allow it to gather up the energy of the third eye to add to that of the smile.

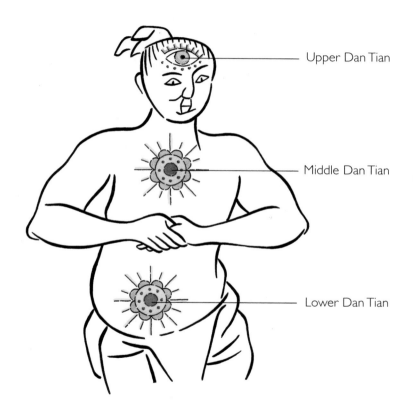

Upper Dan Tian

Middle Dan Tian

Lower Dan Tian

✴ As soon as you feel that the energy has amassed as much third-eye power as possible, let it rise swiftly to a point about six inches above your head. Spin and accumulate the powerful energy of your crown chakra or halo until you can visualize it glowing brilliantly white.

✴ At this stage, take the white fireball of energy back down through your forehead, throat, heart, and spleen, gathering more and more energy into your vortex, and then visualize pouring all that wonderful energy into the sacral chakra, the center of your abdomen. The Chinese call this area (about an inch underneath the center of your lower abdomen) the Dan Tian (see page 203). We refer to it as the physical powerhouse.

✴ Pat your Dan Tian lovingly with your hands, let a smile gently appear on your lips, and open your eyes.

✴ If you wish to do a longer form of this exercise, continue by sending the energy in two directions from the Dan Tian down both legs and into the earth. When the two beams of energy meet at the center of the earth, visualize gathering all the energy the earth can offer you and drawing it back up through the earth, through your legs and into your Dan Tian before patting it into place and opening your eyes with a smile.

The power of water

At this stage of your journey it is useful to get in touch with the energy of water, the element that finds its own level and can be very accommodating, in that it can take on the shape of any container, river, lake, or ocean. This element, at once life-giving and destructive, can wear away any mountain that stands in its path or be so supportive that it allows you to float. In Feng Shui, water energy is associated with your life's purpose, more commonly thought of as your career, so it is a good season to pay serious attention to what you want to achieve in your work.

Water is often thought to be an aid to the sacred. We read in Month 1 how the Hindu goddess Parvati used water from a sacred river to bring her son Ganesh to life (see page 14). Throughout many cultures, rituals involving ceremonial bathing are common. Christian babies are sprinkled with holy water to remember in symbolic form Jesus' own baptism. In Judaism in every local community there is a holy pool, or *mikvah,* for purifying rituals such as the bathing of a bride before her wedding.

People enjoy recreational swimming because of its powers to revitalize and refresh the mind, emotions, and soul as well as strengthen the body.

On water

**This is a beautiful imaginative journey and brings you into a
cosmic relationship with the element of water in all its forms.**

*   Sitting comfortably, imagine that you are by a pool in whose
center is a beautiful fountain that springs, clear and vital and cool. Take
some good, deep breaths and watch the light dance on the water,
shimmering and sparkling with all the colors of the rainbow. Can you
imagine the music of tiny drops and waves spinning, falling, and splashing
as the fountain throws them in glistening arcs into the pool beneath?
Can you sense the fresh clarity of the tiny droplets of water in the sweet
air and feel the almost imperceptible, gentle mist blown by the breeze onto
your skin as you observe the changing surface patterns flow?

*   Knowing that you are the breather of your breaths, the thinker of your
thoughts, the seer of your visions, observe and appreciate your own body,
which is composed mainly (over four-fifths) of water, this wonderful
element whose infinite capacity to transmute its state gives the capacity of
physical life to us all.

*   Take a few more deep breaths and reflect on the process by which the
water has arrived at the point of the fountain. Ride on the rain and be with
it as it sinks into the rich earth, deeper and deeper, marrying its substance
and energy with that of the soil until it meets impervious subterranean
rocks. Then be guided out onto the world's surface into tiny rivulets, which

gather into streams, the streams into rivers, the rivers eventually flowing into the great oceans. Know that in the process, there has been water in abundance to irrigate crops and provide enough refreshment to slake fierce thirsts and bathe tired bodies. Rise up invisibly into the welcoming blue sky as the sun and wind evaporate the crystal-clear water from the rivulets, streams, and rivers, and the seawater from the mighty waves, into vapor. As the clouds form at the edge of the coolness of space, feel the increasing heaviness intensify as rain is created, once more to fall to earth.

✳ Notice how we are drawn together into large groups as we have become interdependent of each other. Architects and builders construct mighty cities in which we live, work, celebrate, and, on occasion, pray. Admire how engineers harness the flowing water from the natural landscape, collect it into reservoirs, direct it into purification processing plants, and then into a system of pipes to deliver the precious supply. The water that springs from fountains and that we use from our taps is part of the cosmic dance of the natural elements. Imagine splashing in the fountain, receiving immense vitality from the surging waters. Now open your eyes.

✳ Reflect on work well done, flowing through your life like a mighty river to the ocean of your society, assessing its creativity, usefulness, and beauty.

On blue and black

According to the discipline of Feng Shui, blue and black are colors that are in tune with winter. The following meditation, which takes only ten minutes, is useful to do whenever you need to experience the particular calmness and wisdom that this season gives. These colors can offer you their magic, so after this meditation you will be in a good frame of mind to make important decisions wisely and philosophically.

* Sitting in the meditative pharaoh position (see page 8), close your eyes, and take three deep breaths, concentrating on the out-breaths and leaving your thoughts behind.

* After the third breath, continue to breathe normally as you imagine walking through a perfect black color for five minutes. Cloak yourself in the energy of knowledge and wisdom that the color black is offering you.

* Now walk out of the enveloping black and into a perfect mid blue. Swim in the energy of perfect blue for another five minutes, absorbing the calmness and peace of mind that it gives.

* After journeying through these colors, return to full awareness and open your eyes.

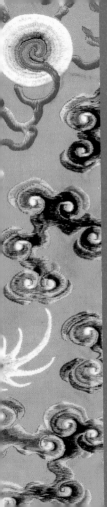

MONTH

11

Trust

Lighting the darkness

Eternal life

Mediumship

Reflecting on spiritual connectedness

Spirit guides and guardian angels

Trust

Members of well-functioning teams need to feel close to each other on the subtle energy level, but conscious trust between team members or a group of family, friends, or colleagues is also essential. An old Chinese legend warns of what can happen if a friend's trust is broken.

The Dragon, the Cockerel, and the Worm

Everybody remembers that, in ancient times, the dragon did not have horns and everybody knows that, in ancient times, the cockerel did have horns, and everybody is aware that only animals with horns are invited to parties in heaven. Every night the cockerel would go to a party in heaven, and every morning on his return his friend the dragon would say:

"Did you have a good time?"

"Yes, fine," the cockerel would reply.

"Can I go? You could lend me your horns, just for one night," the dragon begged.

"No!" the cockerel always retorted.

The dragon kept on pestering him, "Just for one night. It's not fair. I've never been to a party! Oh, please, please, please!"

Eventually, the cockerel began to feel churlish and mean. He went to his friend the worm, who was known for his good advice, and told him that he was beginning to feel quite guilty about not lending the dragon his horns.

And the worm said, "What's the problem? It's only for one night. Does he want to keep them?"

"No, of course he doesn't."

"Well, if you are feeling bad about yourself, lend him your horns for a night."

"Okay, you're right. I will!"

So the cockerel went back and said to the dragon, "Do you absolutely promise it's just for one night?"

The dragon said, "Wow, yeah! Great! Thanks!" He put on the cockerel's horns and went bouncing off to the party.

The dragon had never been to a party in his life. He was so excited, so thrilled, and so enchanted that—although he did really and truly mean to come back when he set off that evening—once he was there he couldn't dream of coming back, because the idea of never going to another party in heaven was too heartbreaking to contemplate. So he never came back. He broke his promise to his friend the cockerel, who had trusted him enough to lend him his precious horns, his passport to heaven.

Which is why today you never see a dragon on earth.

Which is why every morning at sunrise, you hear the cockerel shouting, "Give me back my horns!" to the dragon up in heaven.

This is why then you see him turn around and eat the worm.

Lighting the darkness

Just as in the winter season, every journey has its moments of bleak dreariness. Feng Shui remedies such as tinsel, seasonal plants (Christmas trees, holly, ivy poincettia), bells and sacred music are employed at this time to brighten up the short, cold days and long, dark nights, creating balance and harmony. In Christian countries shopkeepers put up Christmas lights to illuminate the streets and lighten hearts (and hopefully open wallets). People buy Christmas trees and colorful decorations to bring good cheer into their homes. With all these vivid reminders people feel happier and are kinder and more charitable to each other and to those in need in their community. When the festival is over and the decorations come down we must try to remember how we felt and behaved toward each other at Christmas, and make it last. In winter the Hindus celebrate Diwali with fireworks and parties, and Jews remember God's goodness at Hanukkah, the festival of light, and commemorate a historical miracle by lighting candles, singing traditional hymns, and exchanging gifts. In most religions there is a good excuse for giving presents in this season of celebration of life, love, and miracles.

Eternal life

Life is the greatest of all miracles. With more sophisticated resuscitation techniques, doctors are able to pull many people back from the brink of physical death. Some who have clinically died and have been able to be revived have reported the most amazing experiences known as Near-Death Experiences (NDEs). Raymond Moody's book, *Life After Life*, describes his research into the NDE phenomenon in which he interviewed many people who described a process that had striking similarities throughout different genders and cultures. Often people witnessed their own departure from their bodies and heard themselves pronounced dead. After a noise they experienced ineffable calm and traveled through a tunnel into a brilliant light, where they often were greeted by loved ones who they knew had died. A being of light (recognized as whichever deity was relevant to the person's belief system) led them through a review of their life, in which they experienced all the good deeds and the hurts they had caused, from the point of view of the receivers. Some were given a choice to go on into Spirit or to return to life; others were told firmly that it was not their time.

Maybe you already believe in life after life. Even if you do not, use your imagination to consider the consequences of eternal soul life as a reality for you. If the effect of every action you take does indeed have eternal resonance, if each thought and feeling also generates an energy pattern, what steps do you need to take to achieve eternal harmony for your soul?

Mediumship

People with special awareness, known as Spirit mediums, bring to us evidence of the continuation of the soul into the Spirit World by enabling us to have significant, accurate, and detailed conversations with those of our loved ones who have made the natural transition to that wonderful dimension through physical death. They tell us that the souls also describe the near death experience and how, safely arrived in Spirit, they have the opportunity and the choice to learn, progress, develop, and evolve to higher levels.

Professional mediums are not interested in giving messages that cannot be corroborated, or in being fortune-tellers. Their job is to prove that the soul they are in contact with is the person you knew in this life. Spirit mediumship helps and brings comfort to the bereaved by demonstrating the fact that the life of the soul is eternal, and this physical phase of existence is a gift and a learning experience. It is also an opportunity to reach out to each other in order to give and receive love and compassion.

On mediumship

This beautiful way of opening to your own sensitivity of the Spirit World was taught to me by an exceptional medium, Marie Taylor. You may or may not reach contact with the Spirit World, but you should touch into a dimension of sacred stillness, and most people experience feelings of peace, tranquility, and deep joy.

* Sitting comfortably with your eyes closed, begin to breathe slowly, deeply, and easily. Imagine that you are walking down a long staircase until you reach a door at the bottom. On opening the door, the space is full of brilliant light, and there is a crowd of people there. Circulate and meet and chat with some of them.

* After a while, go out of the space and into a beautiful garden. Sit down in the garden and quietly wait until someone you know to be in Spirit comes and sits with you. You may be able to have a conversation with them, or you may just be happy to sit in silent communication with them.

* After a time, come gently back to the here and now and open your eyes.

Reflecting on spiritual connectedness

Reflect on the quality and nature of your connections to the loving souls in the Spirit World. Reflect on the essential, immortal part of you, your soul, the fundamental spiritual energy that is the eternal aspect of you, and how on the soul level you are not separate from everyone and everything in the universe. Imagine the loving energy context from which you journeyed into the physical world at birth and to which you return when the time comes for your natural physical death. Note in your Spirit Diary the new spiritual understandings gained and discuss these with your Soul Friend.

Spirit guides and guardian angels

Many people find it comforting to think about the love that is available to us all in Spirit from the departed souls of loved ones, ancestors, and celestials, those highly evolved energy forms who have never needed to manifest physically, since they already have wisdom and miraculous powers in abundance. It is said that if you acknowledge that you have a guardian angel, and talk joyfully to your angel, your life takes on a new and magical dimension.

Exercise

A letter to your guardian angel

This exercise is to establish communication between you and
your angel. Through your intuition you can then continue
your relationship with your angel for the rest of your life.

* Find a beautiful piece of paper and write a long letter to your
  guardian angel. You do not need to introduce yourself; just use this
  opportunity to communicate as you would to an old and trusted friend
  who knows you very well. Tell your angel about your hopes and dreams and
  what you think about the way your life is going at the moment. Let your
  angel know if you need any celestial help and in what way, and what you
  hope the two of you can achieve together for the good of those you love.
  As you write the letter, imagine that your angel is receiving it and reading it.

MONTH

12

Resting, assessing, planning, giving

Life's purpose

Optimism in action

A pleasure shared

Endings and new beginnings

Resting, assessing, planning, giving

As we approach the end of our journey, we begin to reflect on our experiences, some of which we have enjoyed, and some of which we found more challenging. We realize that all hardships pass eventually and that a new cycle of growth will soon be a reality. Soon spring will return, bringing its hope and comfort.

Many stories, fairy stories, legends, and religious doctrines echo the death and rebirth cycle of this transition of winter to spring. The story of Snow White tells how the wicked queen, her stepmother, who is jealous of Snow White's youth, beauty, and purity, tricks the princess into eating a poisonous apple. The apple sticks in Snow White's throat and causes her to descend into a coma. Everyone thinks she is dead until her prince gives her a farewell kiss, the offending apple is dislodged, and Snow White is revived. Of course, as in all fairy tales, she and the prince marry and live happily ever after.

The Ancient Egyptians built pyramids whose pinnacles would be touched by the sun god, to give souls renewed life and cause the great River Nile to flood at the end of winter, bringing fertility again to their valleys. The Christian story tells of how Jesus was crucified and resurrected with all the joy of miracles that the Easter festival teaches. In Judaism, Passover is celebrated, commemorating the release from bondage into freedom.

Life's purpose

This is a time of year to renew and refresh your soul. In the "Know thyself" exercise from Month 6 (see page 121) you explored the innermost nature of your being and the expression of your needs, hopes, and dreams. As each and every one of us has a life to lead that is unique, and as we each affect everyone else by our actions and our presence, consider now what contribution you can make—some would say the contribution you were destined to make—to this world. From your position on your unique life's path, how can you reach out to your fellows and really make a positive difference? In the Hindu tradition the purpose of each of our lives is called *dharma,* and it encompasses the idea of service to each other, the family of all living things on this planet.

Exploring your dharma

The story of the film *It's a Wonderful Life* is one in which the hero becomes very sad and begins to wish that he had never been born. By some magic, he is given the opportunity to review how the world would have been without his existence. He realizes what significance his life has.

* Sitting comfortably and quietly, reflect on how people, animals, and plants you have known would be today if you had never existed.

* From these insights, realize the effect your presence and actions have had so far in this world and determine how you would like to express your life's purpose in the future and who and what will benefit from your continued presence in the world.

* Develop some ideas about the effects that the lives of those you love have had on you and on others and discuss with them their ideas about their unique dharma.

Your loved ones, friends, and colleagues each have their contribution to your enjoyment of the world and to your coping with difficult times, as you also have for them. As you progress you learn which people you can always rely on to help and support you in challenging times and to share your celebrations in the good times. In the dimension of the Spirit

World, imagine that not only are there guardian angels but also Spirit guides and the souls of your loving ancestors. They are not there to live our lives for us but to build up good energy—to help us make good choices when life exposes us to challenging situations. Ask them a question and listen carefully to their wise, inspirational answers. You may feel that you are in touch with their wisdom or your own inner knowledge of what is right for yourself. Either way, seeking the best possible solution for the highest good is a useful habit to develop.

Thinking of the role that these wonderful beings in the spiritual dimension have in your life, imagine what you could do as an earth angel, very much still here in this world, to help others. Use your awareness of your unique presence to decide how best you can bring happiness and healing into the world. Make a list of all the people who mean something special to you and decide what actions are in your power to enrich their lives.

Attunement

In Feng Shui, the element of winter is water, the direction of the seasonal energy is horizontally floating, with the vibrational quality of the number one. In this meditation you are immersed in winter energy only to emerge peacefully in tune with the world around you, optimally nourished by the natural elements of the season.

* Lie down on the floor, a couch, or your bed and imagine walking through an intense blue color, the vibration of water, knowing that you are on a boat, floating on a vast ocean.

* As you lie there, every cell in your body is systematically being renewed and any ache or pain is being given to the universe for safekeeping. Visit each part of your body in turn, starting with your toes, and observe the renewal process taking place.

* At the end of this meditation, draw in to the shore and disembark onto a beautiful beach. At the edges of the beach tender shoots of spring flowers are almost imperceptibly beginning to show their pale green tips in the grass. Take three deep breaths and imagine that you are breathing into your soul all the energy of the mighty ocean.

* Return to the here and now and open your eyes.

Optimism in action

This is a very good time to be optimistic, but that is not always easy, so you might take the flower essence Sunshine Wattle in the Australian Bush Flower Essences range. This brings the energy of present joy and future hope to your soul. Then tell yourself the story of your life so far, remembering all the contributions you have made to the world.

Unhappy moments are softened in our minds because we can remember that, like the seasons, spring always returns. Positive memory is a lifesaver on occasion, and the story of the death of the Ancient Egyptian god Osiris illustrates this vividly. Osiris was a kind, gentle, and good deity, the husband of the goddess Isis. His brother Seth was eaten up with jealousy, so much so that he killed Osiris and dismembered his body into fourteen pieces. When Isis found out, she grieved for her husband and then decided to take action. She did not rest until she had searched all over the land, found every piece of Osiris, and quietly and with love put him back together again, or re-membered him.

When dark times surround you, use your memories of the light to galvanize you into action. This re-membering will give you faith in the return of the light, giving you the optimism to move on.

Wish list

By projecting good energy into the future, you increase the possibility that what you wish for will be realized. But remember to be careful what you wish for!

✳ At the end of winter, we can look forward to another new year. What do you wish for yourself and for those you care about for the coming year? Make a list or a creative collage or representation.

✳ Next, make a similar wish list for all those on the planet who are suffering war, famine, ill health, or loss.

✳ Place your wish lists in a prominent position within your home, and surround them by a bright red border, because red has the vibration of fire, the element of actualization.

Exercise

Dear me

Deciding on and keeping to good courses of action is so much easier when you commit it to paper.

*   Write a letter to yourself, making promises to undertake your chosen courses of action over the next twelve months. Include in your promises deeds to enhance your own body, mind, and soul, as well as deeds of true service to others. Put the letter in a visible place so that you can notice it frequently, and open it this time next year.

A pleasure shared

It is said that "a pleasure shared is twice the pleasure; a sorrow shared is half the sorrow." Remember that no one can share his or her news without someone else receiving, listening, and accepting. Often this is the undervalued part of the process of sharing but it is such an important and spiritual skill that the last story I have chosen is a traditional tale called "The Little Princess and the Moon." It tells about the importance of knowing how to listen so that someone can reveal to you the wisdom within his or her soul. At times in everyone's life we can experience absolute elation or deep sadness and pain, but even despair is lightened when we feel that someone has listened to us.

The Little Princess and the Moon

Once upon a time there lived a little princess who was loved by absolutely everyone. She was very fortunate, therefore, because everyone tried to please her and grant her her wishes. But one night, the little princess looked up into the sky and decided that she wanted the moon.

Her parents, the king and queen, tried to reason with her:

"You know that you can't have the moon, darling. Nobody can have it. Think of something more attainable!" But the

little princess yearned for the moon. She began to pine and was so sad that it broke everyone's heart. The king and queen made a decree that the person who could make their daughter smile again would be given half their kingdom.

A clown came and did funny tricks, but the princess sighed and wanted the moon.

A horse came who could count and dance and beat time with his hoof and stand on a small box, but the princess cried silently for the moon.

All manner of folk came and told jokes or made funny faces, yet the princess appeared inconsolable.

Then there came a quiet man. He said, "You really do want the moon, don't you!"

The little princess stopped crying and gasped, "Oh, yes!"

He asked, "How big is it?"

She replied, "As big as my thumb. See." And she held her thumb up to the moon.

"Ahum?" said the man.

"And it's all made of silver."

"Ahum?"

"And my parents say that if I took the moon from the sky, the night would be dark. But another would grow in its place."

"Another would grow in its place?"

"Yes! Last month I lost my first tooth and see, there's another one growing in its place. So it will be with the moon."

"And what will you do with the moon?"

"I shall wear it on a little chain around my neck."

So the quiet man made a little moon of silver, and gave it to the little princess to wear around her neck. The little princess smiled and laughed with delight. She was very happy. Because their daughter was so happy, the king and queen were happy once more. Because the monarchs were happy, the whole mood of the country was happy. The quiet man was happy, too, because he now owned half the country, so everybody lived happily ever after.

Endings and new beginnings

Reflect on your year of spiritual development, selecting the moments that have been the most intimately meaningful to you. Celebrate your unique life by creating some ritual, planting a beautiful plant, donating to a charity, or doing some other action of significance to you. Reflect on your spiritual contribution to the life of those around you. Make a representation of your ideas on your life's purpose in your Spirit Diary, and share your thoughts on this and the development of your spiritual awareness throughout the year with your Soul Friend.

As the final days of this year of spirituality come to an end, a new year begins to grow in its place. Just like the moon, the seasons and their miracles will always be with us, and I wish that you, too, will live a magical life spiritually in tune with the natural pulse of the seasons and happily ever after.

Bibliography

Adams, Patch, M.D. *Gesundheit!* Rochester, Vermont: Healing Arts Press, 1998.

Bach, Edward. *The Twelve Healers and Other Remedies.* Saffron Walden, England: C. W. Daniel Co., 1933.

Bandler, Richard, and John Grinder. *The Structure of Magic.* Palo Alto, California: Science and Behavior Books, 1975.

Chopra, Deepak, M.D. *Quantum Healing.* New York: Bantam, 1989.

Cousins, Norman. *Anatomy of an Illness.* New York: W. W. Norton and Co., 1980.

Englesman, Joan. *The Feminine Dimension of the Divine.* Philadelphia: Westminster Press, 1979.

Foundation for Inner Peace. *A Course in Miracles.* Mill Valley, California: Foundation for Inner Peace, 1999.

Gibran, Kahlil. *The Prophet.* London: William Heinemann, 1926.

Holden, Robert. *Happiness Now!* London: Hodder and Stoughton, 1998.

Holden, Robert. *Laughter. The Best Medicine.* London: Thorsons, 1993.

Housden, Roger, and Stephen Hodge, trans. *The Tibetan Oracle.* New York: Harmony Books, 1998.

Lao-tzu. *Tao Te Ching.* Translated by. Richard Wilhelm. London: Arkana, 1985.

Linn, Denise. *Sacred Space.* London: Rider, 1995.

Moody, Raymond A., Jr., M.D. *Life After Life*. Harrisburg, Pennsylvania: Stockpole Books, 1976.

Morford, Mark P. O., and Robert J. Lenardon. *Classical Mythology*. New York: McKay, 1976.

Osborn, Marijane, and Stella Longland. *Rune Games*. London: Routledge and Kegan Paul, 1982.

Pert, Candace. *Molecules of Emotion*. New York: Scribner, 1997.

Remen, Rachel Naomi. "The Search for Healing" in *Healers on Healing*, ed. R. Carlson and B. Shield. Los Angeles: Tarcher, 1989.

Reps, Paul, ed. *Zen Flesh, Zen Bones*. Boston: Charles E. Tuttle Co., 1957.

Robbins, Anthony. *Awaken the Giant Within*. New York: Simon and Schuster, 1992.

Rumi. *Rumi. Hidden Music*. Translated by Azima M. Kolin and Maryam Mafi. London: Thorsons, 2001.

Siegel, Bernie, M.D. *Love, Medicine and Miracles*. New York: HarperPerennial, 1990.

Siegel, Bernie, M.D. *Peace, Love and Healing*. New York: Perennial Library, 1990.

Spear, William. *Feng Shui Made Easy*. San Francisco: HarperSanFrancisco, 1995.

White, Ian. *Australian Bush Flower Essences*. Australia: Bantam Books (Transworld), 1991.

Wilhelm, Richard, trans. *I Ching*. London: Routledge and Kegan Paul, 1951.

Williamson, Marianne. *Illuminata*. New York: Riverhead Books, 1994.

Williamson, Marianne. *Illuminated Prayers*. New York: Simon and Schuster, 1997.

Yoshikawa, Takashi. *The Ki*. New York: St. Martin's Press, 1986.

Resources

Ingrid Collins
The London Medical Centre
144 Harley Street
London W1G 7LD
UK
tel: 44 (0) 20 7935 0023
fax: 44 (0) 20 7935 5972
e-mail: healing@dircon.co.uk

Ingrid is a consultant psychologist, registered spiritual healer, and Feng Shui consultant. She offers soul therapy treatment for individuals, couples, families, staff, and groups.

The Soul Therapy Centre
tel/fax: 44 (0) 20 8883 8562
e-mail: healing@dircon.co.uk
Soul therapy treatment and training center.

The Happiness Project
Elms Court
Chapel Way
Botley
Oxford OX2 9LP
UK
tel: 44 (0) 1865 244 414
fax: 44 (0) 1865 248 825
e-mail: hello@happiness.co.uk
www.happiness.co.uk

Patch Adams, M.D.
Gesundheit! Institute

2630 Robert Walker Place
Arlington
VA 22207
USA
tel: 1 (703) 525 8169

The Anthony Robbins Foundation
9191 Towne Centre Drive
Suite 600
San Diego
CA 92122
USA
tel: 1 (800) 445 8183

The Findhorn Group
Meridian
The Park
Findhorn
Forres
Morayshire AV36 0TZ
UK
tel: 44 (0) 1309 690943
fax: 44 (0) 1309 690933
Spiritual community that also produces
courses, books, and tapes.

The Feng Shui Society
377 Edgware Road
London W2 1BT
UK
e-mail: info@fengshuisociety.org.uk

Peggy O'Hare
Presence and Presents Bookshop
9 Brewers Lane
Richmond Upon Thames
Surrey TW9 1HH
UK
tel/fax: 44 (0) 20 8332 6566
e-mail: pandpohare@msn.com
Sells a large range of books, tapes, and
gift items. Also organizes workshops and
courses.

British Psychological Society
St. Andrews House
48 Princess Road East
Leicester LE1 7DR
UK
tel: 44 (0) 116 254 9586
fax: 44 (0) 116 247 0787

e-mail: mail@bps.org.uk
www.bps.org.uk

Confederation of Healing
Organizations and the British
Alliance of Healing Associations
Secretary: Mr. G. Stockton
40 Cosawes Park Homes
Perranarworthal
Truro
Cornwall TR3 7QS
UK
tel/fax: 44 (0) 1872 865827

Kensington Consultation Centre
2 Wyvil Court
Trenchold Street
London SW8 2TG
UK
tel: 44 (0) 20 7720 7301
fax: 44 (0) 20 7720 7302
enquiries@kcc-international.com
www.kcc-international.com

The Spiritualist National Union
Redwoods
Stansted Hall
Stansted Mount Fitchet
Essex
CM24 8UD
tel: 44 (0) 1279 816363
fax: 44 (0) 1279 812034
e-mail: snu@snu.org.uk
Professional development and
training for spirit mediums of the
highest standard.

ECaP, Exceptional Cancer Patients
(founded by Bernie Siegel, M.D.)
522 Jackson Park Drive
Meadville
PA 16335
USA
tel: 1 (814) 337 8192
fax: 1 (814) 337 0699
e-mail: info@mind-body.org
www.ecap-online.org

Picture Credits

All antique embroidered textile images appear courtesy of Linda Wrigglesworth Ltd., London, copyright © Linda Wrigglesworth, Ltd.

p. 2, 12, 68, 83, 228, 237 Embroidered Souchao hanging depicting birds and flowers in the islands of Penglai. **p. 10, 61** 19th century Manchu woman's embroidered winter robe depicting "the three friends" and shou symbols. **p. 19, 155, 188, 207, 226, 244** 18th century Kesi weave scroll depicting the eight immortals, the three stars of happiness, and the goddess of the West, Xi Wangmu, arriving on a phoenix. **p. 25, 86, 152** Pair of 19th century embroidered chair covers. **p. 26** Late 19th century Manchu woman's gauze silk robe embroidered with lotus and lily pads. **p. 30, 212** Early 19th century Imperial Yellow Empress' chaofu. **p. 38, 72, 75, 92, 128, 215** Front of a Taoist priest's robe embroidered with the Yin-Yang symbol and four of the eight trigrams. **p. 41** Manchu woman's robe woven with butterflies to symbolize happiness. **p. 43, 85, 180** Han Chinese woman's jacket embroidered with roundels of scenes from a play. **p. 46, 77, 247** Military badge of a 2nd rank officer depicting a lion. **p. 49, 89, 138, 141** Celebration hanging from the great hall of a Mandarin house. **p. 50, 115** 19th century Manchu woman's silk embroidered late summer robe. **p. 53, 149, 174** 19th century Han woman's silk robe. **p. 56, 137, 218** Detail of embroidery depicting a dignitary and his wife receiving gifts. **p. 64, 90** 18th century Sino-Tibetan altar frontal embroidered with Buddhist symbols. **p. 67** 19th century Han Chinese sur-coat, embroidered with cicada and peony. **p. 70, 187** Back of a Taoist priest's robe embroidered with four of the eight trigrams, and a mandala of the Universe, sun and moon constellations, and the pagoda from the mountains of Penglai. **p. 97** Detail from an 18th century Korean wedding robe depicting a male and female egret and lotus flowers. **p. 104, 195** 19th

253

Text Credits

Note: Every care has been taken to contact copyright owners. The editor would be pleased to hear from any copyright holders not acknowledged below, and will make corrections in any future edition.

Acknowledgments

My sincere thanks go to my editors, Salima Hirani, Slaney Devlin, and Ljiljana Baird, and to all at MQ Publications, to my friend Linda Wrigglesworth for the beautiful antique embroideries, to my colleagues Adriana Peñalosa-Clarke, Juan Carlos Lema, and Andrew Chevallier, and to my students and clients at the Soul Therapy Centre and the London Medical Centre.

I dedicate this book to my husband, Nick, my mother, Mona, and the memory of my late father, Jack: the three people I love most in this world.

And to God, the celestials, and healing guides of the spirit world.